Great and Manifold

A CELEBRATION OF THE BIBLE IN ENGLISH

COMMEMORATING THE FOUR-HUNDREDTH ANNIVERSARY OF THE FIRST PRINTING OF THE KING JAMES BIBLE

Exhibition & Catalogue by Pearce J. Carefoote

with contributions by

The Most Reverend Thomas Collins

The Reverend Dorcas Gordon

The Most Reverend Colin Johnson

The Reverend Michael Kolarcik, S.J.

The Right Reverend Mark MacDonald

The Very Reverend Bruce McLeod

The Reverend Harvey Self

Rabbi Jonah Chanan Steinberg

The Very Reverend Douglas Stoute

THOMAS FISHER RARE BOOK LIBRARY

UNIVERSITY OF TORONTO   7 FEBRUARY – 3 JUNE 2011

Catalogue and exhibition by Pearce J. Carefoote
General editors Anne Dondertman and Philip Oldfield
Exhibition installed by Linda Joy
Digital Photography by Paul Armstrong
Catalogue designed by Stan Bevington
Catalogue printed by Coach House Press
Cover art: Design binding by Michael Wilcox for a leaf of the Gutenberg Bible.
From a private collection.

LIBRARY AND ARCHIVES CANADA CATALOGUING IN PUBLICATION

Great and manifold : a celebration of the Bible in English : commemorating the four hundredth anniversary of the first printing of the King James Bible / exhibition and catalogue
by Pearce J. Carefoote ; with contributions by Thomas Collins ...[et al.].

Includes bibliographical references.
Catalogue of an exhibition held at the Thomas Fisher Rare Book
    Library, University of Toronto, from Feb. 7 to May 30, 2011.
ISBN 978-0-7727-6105-7

    I. Bible. English—Versions—Authorized—History—Exhibitions.
I. Carefoote, Pearce J., 1961- II. Collins, Thomas Christopher
III. Thomas Fisher Rare Book Library

BS186.G74 2010   220.5'2038   C2010-906968-4

Foreword

The occasion of this celebratory exhibition and catalogue of the English Bible is, of course, the four - hundredth anniversary of the first edition of the King James Bible in 1611. It has often been described as 'the only literary masterpiece ever to have been produced by a committee', but while its influence has been profound and wide-ranging on all the literature written in English since 1611, its importance has reached into and affected the lives of everyone who has come into contact with it. The history of the Bible in English is much longer than four hundred years, as P.J. Carefoote has cogently demonstrated throughout the catalogue, and has involved many languages other than English. The original title-page, and those of all the thousands of later editions, said 'Appointed to be read in Churches' and this admonition, as has been astutely noted by Bruce McLeod, was meant by the translators to be taken literally; pronounced from a lectern or read aloud from an armchair for the full effect of the beauty of this language.

The Thomas Fisher Rare Book Library is privileged to be able to present this exhibition primarily from its own collections and those of the other special collections at the University of Toronto. The reason that our collections are so richly endowed with Bibles is part of the history of the University, which was founded as an amalgamation of theological colleges (with the exception of University College), beginning in 1827. The faculty, students, and supporters of the colleges naturally had many Bibles, which were avidly collected then, as they still are, and many of them have made their way into our collections. The Fisher Library copy of the first edition of the King James Bible was donated by Louis Melzack, a nice ecumenical touch.

This exhibition and catalogue have been enthusiastically supported by the major representatives of all the denominations who conduct teaching programes in the Toronto School of Theology at the University of Toronto and I wish to thank the nine eminent divines who have contributed to the catalogue. A special acknowledgement is due to a private collector in Toronto for the loan of a leaf from the Gutenberg Bible, the first to be printed from moveable type in 1455.

Support for the printing of this catalogue has been generously given by Janet Dewan and Barbara Tangney in memory of their parents, Marian and Harry Ade who were enthusiastic longtime supporters of the Fisher Library. As always, the Friends of the Fisher Library have been of great assistance with their funding as well. The greatest acknowledgement is, of course, to P.J. Carefoote for his many hours of scholarly research and his writing of this catalogue. Amen.

Richard Landon, Director, Thomas Fisher Rare Book Library

Preface

I have a copy of the Bible on my Blackberry. I use it when I travel and sometimes for a quick reference when I'm in a meeting. It's useful, but what I really love is the heft of a beautifully bound leather Bible with pages I can leaf through, see the context of the neighbouring passages, and see how it is set on the page.

I remember my first Bible, given to me by my grandparents at my confirmation. Black, fine calfskin, gilt-edged, the 'Bible paper' - onion-skin thin but not transparent, the text elegantly set out with the words of Jesus in red lettering, the pictures and the maps. It was not like any other book I owned.

That Bible I received at confirmation was the Revised Standard Version. This was what was read in the church of my youth, and the New Revised Standard Version was what we studied at seminary. The New English Bible was handed to me at my ordination. And it is the NRSV that I read and pray with daily and that has formed my scriptural memory.

Except...

> 'In the beginning was the Word ... and the Word was made flesh and dwelt among us, (and we beheld his glory, the glory as of the only begotten of the Father,) full of grace and truth.'

> 'Comfort ye, comfort ye my people.'

> 'And she brought forth her firstborn son, and wrapped him in swaddling clothes, and laid him in a manger.'

> 'And now abideth faith, hope, charity, these three; but the greatest of these is charity.'

Except . . . we know the King James Version for all the really memorable passages: the festival readings of Christmas and Easter, the anthems that I sang in choir and the plethora of Handel's *Messiahs* that have embedded themselves in our collective consciousness.

How many times have I stood at a hospital bedside and recited the magisterial KJV translation of the sonorous Hebrew of the 23rd Psalm! It's not the modern words that I quote, but: 'The Lord is my shepherd; I shall not want. He maketh me to lie down in green pastures: he leadeth me beside the still waters.' Often the family joins in from memory. And from some depths of stirred memory, those words form on the dying patient's lips. 'Yea, though I walk through the valley of the shadow of death, I will fear no evil: for thou art with me...'

The words sear themselves into our unconscious, and form our souls and hearts.

It is not an exaggeration to say that the culture of the English-speaking world has been deeply shaped, consciously or not, by this English text. A quick scan of Bartlett's *Book of Quotations* reveals almost sixty pages of entries from The Bible (KJV) that have found their way into common parlance. Language shapes the way we perceive the world and make sense of what is around us. It gives us a vehicle to communicate our own understanding with others. For four hundred years, the KJV has been a backbone of that shared world in English-speaking places. And as the explorers, public servants and entrepreneurs of the English (and other competing European nations) travelled around the globe, so did the Bible. It was a source of missionary activity, of inculcating morals, linking homesick émigrés to home parishes, teaching English to 'natives' and children, organising and legitimising systems of governance. It transmitted a whole culture.

We define ourselves by the stories we tell. For centuries, these were our common stories, told in a particular cadence and rhetorical elegance. People who have never heard of Shakespeare or one of his plays, who have not delved into the great body of English literature, have read - and have had read to them - this text. And the literati have had their imaginations and their allusions - aural and visual - enriched by the vocabulary, the images, and the cadences that these extraordinary translators chose to convey the ancient stories of God's interactions with a particular people in a vernacular that soon became the world's *lingua franca*. Even today, the Bible in modern translation has become a vehicle for English-as-a-second-language instruction.

8

It is hard to imagine today the intensity with which people viewed the early vernacular Bible. It was a political as much as a religious act - if there could be a difference in the two in an earlier age! A translator whose work influenced the KJV translation was declared a heretic after his death, his bones dug up, and burned. The KJV was produced by the decision and under the protection of a king, and part of its purpose was to create a religious (and a political and social) cohesion within a realm that was still trying to fend off foreign aggressors and internal religious conflicts. When the English Bibles were first required by law to be placed in parish churches, they were chained to the lecterns so they wouldn't be stolen!

We celebrate four hundred years of this exceptional text. We give thanks for these masters. Over the centuries, there have been revisions and corrections as new information has been found, and new translations as the English language has evolved. The work of translation into the vernacular of other cultures to which the Bible has been brought continues to this day. But the principles enunciated in the original work of the KJV translators have always been maintained: to produce authoritative and trustworthy texts based on the earliest manuscripts, and with the benefit of the most current scholarly studies; for the use of those who would employ this book as Scripture, as the Word of God addressed to them, with the power to shape the lives they live; or for others to explore the basic sources that inform their neighbour's beliefs.

The Most Reverend Colin R. Johnson, Archbishop of Toronto and
Metropolitan of Ontario, Anglican Diocese of Toronto, October 2010

THE

Holy Bible,

CONTAINING THE

OLD TESTAMENT

AND

THE NEW:

Tranflated out of the

Original Tongues,

AND

With the former TRANSLATIONS

Diligently Compared and Revifed,

By His MAJESTY's Special Command.

❖❖❖❖❖❖❖❖❖❖❖❖❖❖❖❖❖❖❖❖❖❖❖❖❖❖❖❖

APPOINTED TO BE READ IN CHURCHES.

❖❖❖❖❖❖❖❖❖❖❖❖❖❖❖❖❖❖❖❖❖❖❖❖❖❖❖❖

CAMBRIDGE,

Printed by *JOHN BASKERVILLE,* Printer to the UNIVERSITY.

M DCC LXIII.

CUM PRIVILEGIO.

Introduction

Monday, 16 January 1604. It is not a date that echoes with obvious meaning down the corridors of time; and yet, few others hold such import for the development of English literature and language. For it was on that day that King James 1 of England, after a series of heated exchanges with representatives of the Puritan and more Catholic wings of the Church of England, ordered that a new Bible be produced for his people. It is not known precisely on which day in 1611 the first copies were printed. What is known is that it was not warmly received, at least initially, in many quarters for reasons that will be explained later. Within a fairly short space of time, however, its mellifluous prose and poetry became synonymous with Sacred Writ itself, so much so, that down to the present day there are many who would assert, without the least sense of irony, that God's Word was revealed in neither Hebrew nor Greek, but in late Elizabethan English.

Any first-year divinity student can explain that the Bible, as it is understood by Jews and Christians, is not divine dictation. It is believed, rather, to be the product of inspiration and revelation; a narrative history of humans reaching out to what they have perceived to be the Divine around and in them, the Divine touching them back. Its origins are hidden in the mists of earliest Middle Eastern civilization, where a vivid oral tradition still prevailed over the written text. But in the final analysis, it is communication, and communication requires language. The language enfolding this particular narrative is considered sacred in every culture that continues to tell the ancient story.

For English speakers, however, the King James Version of the Bible has assumed pride of place, even among those for whom the Scriptures are considered neither inspired nor revealed. One of the reasons for this is because, as Winston Churchill observed, 'the scholars who produced this masterpiece ... forged an enduring link, literary and religious, between the English-speaking people of the world.'

The King James (or 'Authorized') Version helped to give the Anglo-Saxon world a common set of expressions that were, quite simply put, beautiful. The phraseology had rhythm and cadence; the vocabulary was chosen not only to inform accurately, but to elevate the reader. George Bernard Shaw described the supreme accomplishment of the book in this way:

> The translation was extraordinarily well done because to the translators what they were translating was not merely a curious collection of ancient books written by different authors in different stages of culture, but the word of God divinely revealed through His chosen and expressly inspired scribes. In this conviction they carried out their work with boundless reverence and care and achieved a beautifully artistic result ... They made a translation so magnificent that to this day the common human Britisher or citizen of the United States of North America accepts and worships it as a single book by a single author, the book being the Book of Books and the author being God.

Shaw here hints at the danger of bibliolatry which endures to this day in some quarters, but his point should not be lost. This was the book which, together with the works of Shakespeare, taught English-speakers how to think, comfort one another, speak, and write well.

Even those who have never opened its covers have likely uttered its elegant axioms. 'Am I my brother's keeper?'; 'An eye for an eye'; 'Our daily bread'. These and many more expressions are so deeply woven into the fabric of English culture and literature that they have become part of our collective consciousness. Yet, though they were preserved by King James's translators, these rich phrases had in fact already entered the language almost one hundred years earlier, through the auspices of the reformer, scholar, and linguist, William Tyndale (d. 1536). As important as the King James Bible is within the world of letters, therefore, it should not be studied in isolation.

With his ears attuned to the sonority of language, St Jerome (d. 420) set the standard for Biblical translation when he embarked upon the writing of the Latin Vulgate Bible over one thousand years earlier. Like the King James translators, he approached the Scriptures as literature as well as divine revelation, referring more often to classical poetry and prose than to the Scriptures themselves in the prefaces to each book of his Bible. His brief analyses of the Book of Psalms, Isaiah, Jeremiah, and Lamentations are as much commentaries on style, metre, and layout as they are reflections on Sacred Writ. Within the context of English Biblical literature, the King James Version is perhaps the most beloved and best-known example of the genre, but it is far from the sole monument that so many think it to be. It had noble predecessors, stretching back to the Anglo-Saxon glosses of the Lindisfarne Gospels written in the eighth century; Tyndale, Coverdale, the Great Bible, and Geneva in the sixteenth century; and it has had so many successors that they are almost too numerous to count. Some are worthy testimonials to the efforts of great scholars; many others less so. While this exhibition marks the four-hundredth anniversary of the first printing of the King James Bible, therefore, it is actually a celebration of the Bible in English, in its many and varied forms.

The Problem of Translation

The translation of the Bible has always been a challenging, if frequently thankless, task. At the request of Pope Damasus, for example, St Jerome undertook the revision of the Old Latin Gospels around the year 382. With one eye cast on the 'pure' Greek texts, he crafted a new copy of the Scriptures in the 'vulgar' or common tongue - hence, the Vulgate. The project would eventually take him about twenty-four years to complete. In the end, he revised both Testaments in a manner that, while sympathetic to the old beloved Latin versions, still caused a certain amount of popular discord over some of the translations themselves. Tampering with the sacred words could mean tampering with their efficacy in both the spiritual and temporal realms, and so many of the faithful, then as now, were loath to see traditional renderings of memorable passages altered. Nevertheless, the Vulgate, as translated by Jerome and others from the ancient Greek, Latin, Hebrew, and Aramaic sources flourished and remains the official Biblical text for the Roman Catholic Church; indeed, it was *the* Bible for all Western Christians for a thousand years until the Reformation of the sixteenth century. As David Howlett states, 'It's the one book we all know they all knew'.

The story of the English Bible really begins with the iconic Lindisfarne Gospels which were created in Northumbria around the year 721. They represent one of the most accurate copies of the Vulgate in existence, having been transcribed from particularly reliable southern Italian manuscripts that may originally have been edited at the monastery of Cassiodorus in the sixth century. About the year 950, Aldred, a priest at Chester-le-Street and guardian of the Gospels, added a running Anglo-Saxon translation over almost every line of the Latin text, thereby making the first essentially complete English version of the Gospels, a feat predating the composition of *Beowulf* by some fifty years. The first full English translation of the entire Vulgate would have to wait, however, until the late fourteenth century when the followers of John Wycliffe (d. 1384), popularly known as the Lollards, produced numerous contraband copies, large numbers of which were destroyed almost as soon as they appeared. Nevertheless, some two hundred and fifty copies have been preserved in at least two editions, so that the so-called 'Lollard Bible' accounts for the single largest instance of survival of any medieval English text. Although it was constantly challenged and eventually condemned in 1407, the fact that extensive quotations from the Lollard Bible appear regularly in sermons throughout the Lancastrian period demonstrates that it continued to influence the English church in the era leading up to the Reformation.

The Vulgate was, of course, also the first book to appear in print in the West, issued by Gutenberg's press in the mid-1450s. It became, not surprisingly, one of the most popular publications of the incunable era, not to mention among the most complicated to typeset. The reason for this was that the educated public not

14

only wanted the Biblical texts, but the commentaries that went along with them, all neatly laid out on the same page. None was perhaps as complex as those late fifteenth-century Bibles containing the *Postilla* of Nicholas of Lyra (ca. 1270-1349) together with the *Additiones* of Paul of Burgos. In time, the intricate layout squeezed most of the Biblical text right off the page in favour of the medieval glosses, causing the early reformers to demand a return to the purity of the Biblical text alone, with no human intervention save chapter headings. While these glosses may have disappeared, the temptation to editorialize upon the Scriptures did not, as the margins of the Geneva and Douai-Rheims Bibles demonstrate.

But was the Vulgate, as noble as it was, the best place to start when making an accurate vernacular translation of the Scriptures? The answer to this question generally depended on one's ecclesiology, since those who ardently supported the authority of Rome (like the priests of the English College at Rheims), tended to agree that Jerome's inspired translation was the *locus classicus.* Scholars like Desiderius Erasmus (d. 1536) and Jacques Lefèvre d'Etaples (d. 1536), however, who insisted on the return *ad fontes* for all academic disciplines, generally thought not. It is understandable, therefore, that when the Humanist movement finally took root in England, with its emphasis on the 'return to the sources', exponents like William Tyndale (d. 1536) who assumed the arduous task of Biblical translation on his own, usually turned to manuscript and print versions of the Scriptures in the original Hebrew and Greek. For them, there was no point in using the Vulgate, since that would merely mean making a translation from a translation.

The first and most important printed source used in the production of vernacular translations was the Complutensian Polyglot Bible of Cardinal Ximénes de Cisneros (1436-1517) which was printed between 1502 and 1517. This enormous monument to both the Humanist skill and the typographer's art presented the ancient texts of the Scriptures in numerous columns and included, among other sources, the Hebrew Old Testament together with the Greek Septuagint, as well as the first printed Greek text of the New Testament. Unfortunately, exactly which manuscripts were consulted by the redactors in putting together these influential volumes remains something of a mystery. The second important source, especially for New Testament scholars, was Erasmus's 1516 *Novum Instrumentum* which was the first serious Latin translation of the New Testament based on the original Greek text since St Jerome. Erasmus's 1519 revision which was retitled *Novum Testamentum*, proved to be even more influential.

The translation of the Bible specifically into English, however, was a controversial and unlawful act. For that reason, among all of the European nations, England would be the last to have a legal, printed copy of the Scriptures in its native tongue. The reason for this was that there had long been an association between literacy and heresy in England dating back to the early fifteenth century and the Lollards. According to the seventh clause of *Constitutiones* of 1409, written by Archbishop Thomas Arundel of Canterbury (1353-1414), the translation of any part of the Bible into English was explicitly forbidden. Violation of the law resulted in excommunication, a charge of heresy, and the possibility, if convicted, of being burnt alive in keeping with the 1401 edict of King Henry IV (1366-1413), *De heretico comburendo*. Nevertheless, the translation and reading of the Bible in English continued secretly throughout the fifteenth century, with the Bishop of Chichester, Reginald Peacock (d. 1460) complaining that laymen would no longer accept the word of their parish priests but 'would fetch and learn their faith at the Bible of Holy Scripture, in a manner as it shall hap them to understand it.'

It was possible to obtain an Episcopal licence to own and read an English manuscript Bible even before the Reformation, but such a policy was actually counterproductive. By confining legal access to the English Scriptures to the wealthy, it caused many in the lower classes, especially in the northwest of the kingdom, to favour those officially declared heretics. It certainly helped prepare the ground for the more radical reformers that would emerge during and after the reign of Henry VIII. Henry himself was essentially a conservative in matters of religion who firmly resisted an English translation of the Scriptures. He became so incensed that ordinary people were discussing the Bible among themselves in churches and public houses that on 6 March 1529 he issued a proclamation against the reading of unlicensed books, directed specifically at the English Scriptures which by that time were being imported from the Continent. Even after his break with Rome, Henry issued a proclamation in 1539 limiting the exposition and reading of Scripture to graduates of Oxford or Cambridge. In 1543 he passed an Act forbidding the reading of the Bible by 'women, artificers, journeymen, servingmen of the rank of yeoman and under, husbandmen, and laborers'; and while noblemen and women were permitted to study the sacred text in English privately, they were forbidden from reading it aloud to commoners.

The translation of any document, especially a book as invested with meaning as the Bible, is a dangerous enterprise since every act of translation is also an act of interpretation. Tyndale's decision to render the Greek words *ekklesia* as 'congregation' rather than 'church' and *presbyter* as 'elder' rather than 'priest', for example, was as much an ideological statement as it was semantic choice. It is primarily for this reason that both Church and State have tried to control the process throughout the centuries. It has been erroneously reported that Sir Thomas More, perhaps Tyndale's greatest nemesis, opposed the translation of the Bible into English; in fact, it was its *unauthorized* translation that was repugnant to him since, according to his philosophy, the Bible was first and foremost the Church's book.

In the end, however, the Scriptures were translated into English; they were revised, and daily proclaimed from pulpits the breadth and length of the kingdom during Henry's reign, whetting the appetite for a freer access to the Scriptures that came with the brief administration of his son, Edward VI (1537-1553). With the succession of Mary I (1516-1558), Bibles were once again removed from the parishes, though the reading of the English Bible was, in and of itself, not condemned. By then, it was the *Protestant* origin of the Bible that was suspect, no longer its language. Mary's Archbishop of Canterbury, Reginald Pole (1500-1558), was an evangelically-minded prelate who, as early as 1555, had expressed his fervent desire that a new English translation of the New Testament be prepared for Catholics in England, though he remained suspicious of 'indiscriminate Bible-reading' by the laity.

As the reign of Elizabeth I (1533-1603) moved irresistibly towards that of her successor, James I, pride in the English language grew along with a new-found patriotism, and the English Bible played a major role in the emergence of that phenomenon. Nevertheless, a certain apprehension associated with making the Scriptures so easily accessible to the ordinary reader endured in both Protestant and Catholic camps. Explanatory marginal notes were added by the Geneva and Rheims editors to ensure that Bible owners interpreted the sacred text according to the intention of the translators, who seemed hesitant to trust their readers' own intellectual judgments. The Roman *Index librorum prohibitorum* of 1564 declared that 'if the Sacred Books are permitted everywhere and without discrimination in the vernacular, there will by reason of the boldness of men arise therefrom more harm than good'. These concerns appear to have been justified in the light of some of the excesses displayed by religious radicals in the sixteenth and seventeenth centuries. Thomas Hobbes, writing in 1668 in the wake of the English Civil War agreed. 'For after the Bible was translated into English', he observed, 'every man, nay every boy and wench that could read English, thought they spoke with God Almighty, and understood what he said, when by a certain number of chapters a day they had read the Scriptures once or twice over, the reverence and obedience due to the Reformed Church here, and to the Bishops and Pastors therein, was cast off, and every man became a judge of religion and an interpreter of the Scriptures to himself.'

Reading the lofty prose of Tyndale, Coverdale, Geneva, Douai-Rheims, or the King James one can easily forget the revolutionary character of much of 'the Book'. As beautiful or odd or historically conditioned as its sentiments may at times be, the English Bible is a document that has the power to 'comfort the afflicted and afflict the comfortable'. 'Great men are not always wise.' 'He hath put down the mighty from their seats, and exalted them of low degree.' 'Blessed are the meek, for they shall inherit the earth.' 'Woe unto you that are rich!' With statements such as these, it is perhaps not surprising that so many in Church and State spent so much time attempting to prevent the farmer's wife or the ploughboy from reading them. Hence the overriding importance of the Church insisting on having an authorized version to help build consensus in the midst of so much opinion and self-interpretation.

The myriad versions and editions of the English Bible that have appeared over the past five hundred years should today be seen, for the most part, as complements to one another rather than as rivals. Some lend themselves better to personal meditation; others to public worship; still others to study and teaching; and a very few belong to the world of fine literature. In the middle of the nineteenth century, when the contest between Catholic and Protestant versions of the Bible had reached its zenith, the Roman Catholic Bishop of Philadelphia and Bible translator Francis Kenrick perhaps best summarized the grudgingly respectful relationship of these contending versions of Scripture to one another:

> *In adopting occasionally the words and phrases of the Protestant version, I have followed the example of others who have, from time to time revised the Rhemish translation. It is not to be regretted, that whilst we point to errors which need correction, we acknowledge excellencies which we are free to imitate, thus diminishing the asperity of censure by the tribute which we willingly render to literary merit. I avail myself, however, of the testimony of those who are outside the pale of the Church only by way of acknowledgment on their part, or in matters purely critical, in which they have brought their stories of erudition and their natural acuteness of mind to the vindication of the sacred text.*

The title of this exhibition, 'Great and Manifold', is drawn from the opening words of the dedicatory preface of the King James Bible of 1611, which offer hearty thanks for the succession of the Stuart King to the throne of England. As important as that event was to the life of the nation, the main concern of the translators was to remind the King that the Word was still living and active, an 'inestimable treasure which excelleth all the riches of earth'. 'Great and manifold' have been the ways in which the English Scriptures have appeared for almost half a millennium now - and not only the Church, but the home, the law courts, the theatre, and literature are the beneficiaries.

The thyr
de figure

every one of them . And it was sayde vnto
them that they shulde reste for a lyttle season
vntyll the nomber of their felowes/ and bre
thre/ and of them that shulde be kylled as they
were/were fulfylled.

esa.ij.b.
ozee.v.b.
luc.xviij

And I behelde when he opened the sixte se O
ale/and loo there wos a grett erth quake and
the sunne was as blacke as sacke clothe made
of heare. And the mone weyed even as bloud:
and

The.v. fi
gure.

From the Tyndale Bible (1534).

20

The Ancient Sources
of the English Bible

'The Blessed Holy One looked into the Torah and created the world.' So says a rabbinic teaching from the first centuries of the Common Era. In that Jewish view, the cosmos itself is a work of translation, a transcription of divine word into material reality and life. The Scriptures, in rabbinic exegesis, are not merely a tissue of laws and stories; they are warp and weft in the fabric of the world, a verbal manifestation of the wisdom that was with God in the beginning. Scripture, in Jewish tradition, is the 'well of living waters' of the Song of Songs and the 'tree of life' of the Proverbs. 'Turn her over and turn her over,' says one Talmudic adage, 'for everything is in her.'

Jewish religion abounds in interpretation, but Scripture, in its original languages of Hebrew and Aramaic, is the ground of all. God *speaks* the world into being in the first lines of Genesis, and centuries of Jewish interpreters regard those Scriptural lines as nothing less than the world-making words themselves. Judaism today is not the religion of our ancient Israelite ancestors; yet it is the product of many lifetimes dedicated to wrestling with their textual legacy to us, letter by letter. Over time the sacred words become the vehicles for readings that remake their meanings, sometimes radically; yet such interpretive *chutzpah,* to use a Jewish term for the vital audacity, trusts in the generative depths of the Biblical word.

Today, with a global perspective and inclusive values, it is less comfortable to say that the world was created in Hebrew. If we believe that each human being is an essential reflection of the divine, and bears equal responsibility for the state of that reflection in our world, then it is untenable to privilege one people's language over all the rest as a solitary key to God's own thought. The myriad ways in which the

Bible is read the world over, testify to the insistent originality and variety of human spirit, which blessedly even 'the word of God' cannot subdue. Today so many of us look into these Scriptures and create.

Yet for myself, as a Jew, ultimately there can be no translation. Though I use English in teaching, my Scriptures must forever speak to me in their own original words if I am to be their Jewish teacher. Otherwise I might not understand how Wisdom's claim in Proverbs 8:22, that she, 'Wisdom', was created as the *'first'* (in Hebrew, the *resheet*) of God's works, opens the door to the rabbinic reading in which God looked into the Torah, into these words of wisdom, and, as their first exegete, allowed them to guide the creation of our world, thus fulfilling the very first word of Genesis to its Hebrew letter - not merely 'In the beginning', as we are wont to translate, but *be-resheet*, '*With* the *first*,' that is, *with wisdom*, God created . . . And that was just the first word.

Rabbi Jonah Chanan Steinberg, Associate Dean,
Rabbinical School of Hebrew College, Newton Centre, Massachusetts

1   *Codex Torontonensis.* Constantinople? Circa 1070.

This small Greek manuscript was most likely transcribed at Constantinople around the year 1070. The four Gospels compose the main portion of the volume, with the last thirty-five leaves containing the synaxarium and menology (essentially the martyrology) of the Eastern Orthodox Church. The New Testament was originally written in a common form of Greek known as *'koine'*, and it was to volumes such as this one that the Renaissance humanists turned in their quest to provide the first modern vernacular copies of the Christian Scriptures. The binding of the book is essentially contemporaneous, with black leather over wooden boards. The text is written on coarse, thick vellum in a Greek minuscule script which displays Syrian influence; decoration, though restrained, is colourful with four partially illuminated headpieces in the Byzantine style at the beginning of each Gospel. Interestingly, the story of the woman caught in adultery (John 7:53-8:11) is omitted from the main text, but is supplied by a thirteenth-century hand in the margin. This purposeful omission reflects the fact that as late as the eleventh century there was unease with the authenticity of this particular Gospel story which does not appear in the earliest manuscripts of the New Testament and certainly does not originally belong to the Gospel of John. In fact some ancient New Testaments actually place it after Luke 21:38. Brown notes that the pericope does not have any evident Johannine style, and may have been inserted in the third century as an illustration of Jesus' upcoming statement, 'I pass judgment on no one' (John 8:15). The story is certainly more in keeping with Luke's general concern for women and the marginalized of society. The critical process of determining which Greek families of texts, with their divergent readings, should form the basis for modern recensions of the Scriptures led to the development of the *Textus Receptus*, the printed editions of the Greek New Testament which appeared in the late Renaissance and provided the translation base for Luther, Tyndale, and other Reformation-era Biblical scholars. The Gospels presented here have their own unique internal structures with Matthew divided into sixty-eight chapters, Mark into forty-eight, Luke into eighty-three, and John into eighteen. The Codex was purchased from an English antiquarian book dealer by the Toronto Anglican priest and scholar, Henry Scadding (1813-1901) about 1890. Scadding in turn bequeathed the book, together with his whole library, to the University of Toronto upon his death. This particular volume formed part of the exhibition commemorating the tercentenary of the King James Bible sponsored by the Upper Canada Bible Society held from 13-25 February 1911 in Toronto. It has the added distinction of being the first Greek manuscript of the four Gospels to have been brought to Canada.

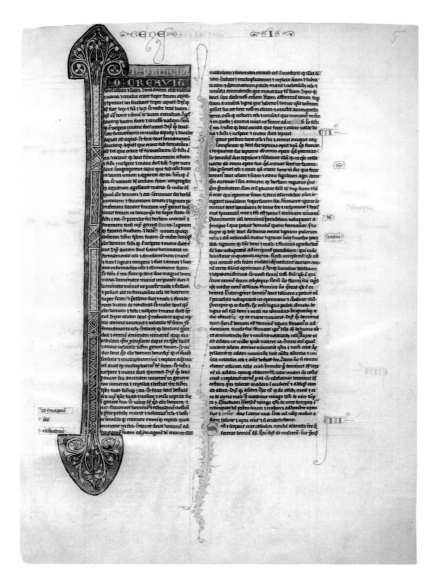

2   *Biblia latina.* Diocese of Canterbury. Circa 1220-1228.

This Vulgate Bible was transcribed and illuminated in the diocese of Canterbury between the years 1220 and 1228. Although the text block was cropped during an eighteenth-century rebinding, the basic size and minuscule script seen here were typical of those single-volume 'pandects' preferred by the new mendicant orders of the Franciscans and Dominicans. The dramatically cramped writing (which was noted as a novelty even in its own day) and almost impossibly thin parchment allowed for the condensing of the entire Scriptures into a single volume. Previous to the thirteenth century, the Bible rarely existed as one book, and could often be found in as many as eight or nine large, separate tomes with one volume dedicated solely to the Pentateuch, a second to the historical books, a third to the Prophets, and so forth. For itinerant preachers, these magnificent and spacious multi-volume sets were highly impractical, leading to the development of the single-volume format of the Bible common today. Another interesting feature of this manuscript is the sequence in which the Biblical books are arranged since they do not completely correspond with the standard order found in modern Bibles. The Wisdom literature, for example, appears at the end of the Old Testament, while the Pauline epistles and Hebrews come immediately before the book of Revelation in the New. This is perhaps not as surprising as it may seem, since the thirteenth century was also the era when the canonical order of the Biblical books was being finally established. Noteworthy for its absence is the book of Psalms, which was often kept as a separate volume owing to its frequent usage in the course of the canonical day. Single-volume Bibles such as these took on iconic status, becoming objects of veneration in and of themselves, carried aloft in processions as well as in battles. This manuscript once belonged to the Collegium Amplonianum at Erfurt and was bought by Lothar Franz von Schönborn (1655-1729), Archbishop of Mainz, in 1725.

On loan from a private collection.

3   *Biblia latina.* Italy (Bologna?). Last quarter 13th century.

The most striking feature about this late thirteenth-century Vulgate Bible is its larger, more rounded script and opulent decoration. Each book opens with a magnificently illuminated historiated initial, accompanied by pen flourishes and arabesques that extend down the length of the page, some including grotesques as shown here at the beginning of the book of Proverbs. The ornamentation bears some similarity to the work of the master illuminator, Jacopino da Reggio, who worked in Italy between the years 1265 and 1300. Blue is the predominant colour, with particularly bright and rich gold leaf. Beyond its sumptuous adornment, however, this Bible bears witness (along with the Canterbury Bible) to one of the most important technical developments in the history of the Bible as a book, for it was in this century that standardized chapter numbering was introduced, probably by Stephen Langton (d. 1228) when he was a lecturer at the University of Paris. As noted with the Codex Torontonensis, previous to this innovation, chapter divisions were generally idiosyncratic and often locally determined. It was only with the arrival of large numbers of international students to the new universities that a standardized text, like this one, became necessary. Peculiarities with regard to the canonical order persist in this manuscript, however, with the Acts of the Apostles, for example, following Hebrews and preceding the Catholic epistles. With the exception of coins, more Bibles survive from the thirteenth century than any other artifact. As with the Canterbury Bible, this volume was rebound by Kling for Lothar Franz von Schönborn, Archbishop of Mainz in the eighteenth century.

On loan from a private collection.

4   *Liber Quattuor Evangelistarum.* Avignon? ca. 1220.

This thirteenth-century Gospel book is an excellent example of the plain, unembellished manuscript that would be more commonly found in the hands of ordinary clerics. According to Christopher de Hamel, it originally belonged either to a Franciscan or Dominican house at Avignon, but certainly formed part of the Maurist monastic library of St-André at Avignon by the seventeenth century. Written in an uneven Gothic minuscule script on parchment, the book is also a fine example of medieval scribal arts. The edge of the pages retain the pricking marks used to guide the original ruling which is still clearly visible on the displayed pages. The only decoration is the larger red capitals used at the beginning of the books, prologues, and divisions. The manuscript does not appear to have been affected by Parisian standardization efforts, since the chapters remain unnumbered according to any system. In fact, the syntax and word order in several places agree with the Old Latin Bible that predated Jerome's Vulgate, which was not as unusual as one might think for a manuscript of such a late date. The English monk Alcuin (d. 804), on the orders of Charlemagne, had assumed responsibility for the production of a more standardized version of Jerome's Vulgate to replace the numerous manuscript variants still in circulation throughout the Holy Roman Empire at that time; nevertheless, it took centuries for it to achieve general acceptance. It was only with the establishment of the universities in the thirteenth century that the 'Alcuin Bibles' finally became the ordinary text of the scholastic world. It was not until the Biblical revisions of Popes Sixtus v (1520-1590) and Clement viii (1536-1605), however, that these variant readings were finally harmonized in what became the official text of the Roman Catholic Church.

5   Torah, Nevi'im, Ketuvim. Toledo, 1307.

According to its colophon, this manuscript copy of the Hebrew Scriptures was written in Toledo, Spain, in the month of Kislev, 5068 (December 1307 c.e.) by Yosef ben Yehudah ben Mervas for Mosheh ben Yosef Yehudah ha-Nasi. The books follow the usual Jewish order, with the exception that the Book of Chronicles precedes Psalms. The *Masorah gedolah* and *Masorah ketanah* are included in the margins. By the High Middle Ages, Spain had come to be considered home to the finest Hebrew manuscripts in Europe, with the scribes of Toledo attaining so high a standard of accuracy that Spanish Jews felt little need to use the new printing press once it had been invented. While some printed Jewish books appeared in Spain before the expulsion of the community in 1492, the printing of the Hebrew Scriptures was principally undertaken at the end of the fifteenth century in northern Italy where humanists had embraced the study of the ancient Biblical languages. In

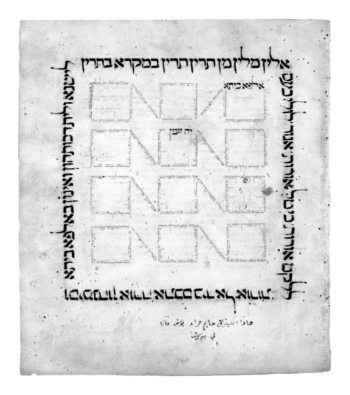

England, the Jews remained a banned population in the sixteenth century and, as a result, scholars there were more suspicious of Hebrew and its influence in the schools. By the second quarter of the sixteenth century, therefore, William Tyndale was one of those very few intellectuals both willing and able to provide a translation of the Old Testament directly from its original tongue. On 17 January 1530 his translation of the first five books of the Bible, the Pentateuch, was printed at Antwerp, and introduced to the English language such resonant phrases as 'Let there be light, and there was light'. Tyndale, whose 1534 New Testament is also on display in this exhibition, demonstrated that he was not only an accomplished scholar but a poet, for he translated the Hebrew in both a lyrical and technically accurate manner.

6   *Biblia latina, cum postillis Nicolai de Lyra et expositionibus Guillelmi Britonis in omnes prologos S. Hieronymi et additionibus Pauli Burgensis replicisque Matthiæ Doering.* Venice: Nicolaus Jenson, 1481.

The most striking characteristic of many incunable Bibles like this one is their complicated page layout. They have been described as a *tour de force* of the printer's art with the Biblical text in large print surrounded by a traditional gloss, beneath which are the *Postilla* or 'notes' of Nicholas of Lyra (d. 1349), followed by the objections of Paul of Burgos (a converted rabbi who took exception to Nicholas's emphasis on Hebrew interpretation), underneath which are the criticisms of Matthias Döring (d. 1469) in Nicholas's defence. Nicholas was one of the few Hebraists to emerge in the later Middle Ages, and in his day he was criticized for 'judaizing' the Scriptures. His *Postilla* or 'notes' show a thorough understanding of the Jewish exegetes, especially Rashi (1040-1105), and it was principally through Nicholas that the Jewish interpretations of the Old Testament were introduced to Christian theologians. Luther was especially influenced by his commentary, prompting the coining of the Latin adage, *'Si Lyra non lyrasset, Luther non saltasset'* meaning, 'Had Lyra not played, Luther could not have danced'. This Venetian imprint represents the first time the *Biblia latina* was printed in combination with Nicholas's extensive reflections. While the reformers were endebted to his insights, they eventually rejected the addition of commentary to the Biblical text in favour of a page relatively unencumbered by marginalia, allowing the Word to speak for itself.

7   *Novum Testamentum omne: multo quam antehac diligentius ab Erasmo Rotero-damo recognitu.* Basel: Johann Froben, 1519.

For humanists like Erasmus, the return to the sources was linked to the search for truth and accuracy. When compared with the original Greek text, it became readily apparent, even to the Church hierarchy of the day, that the Vulgate of St Jerome, though excellent in many ways, also contained numerous inaccuracies. In 1511, therefore, Erasmus began the monumental task of retranslating the New Testament, and in 1516 his *Novum Instrumentum* first saw the light of day. It was not without its own errors, however, and so this 1519 edition represents the improved, corrected New Testament in Greek and Latin which Luther would use as the basis for his great 1522 German New Testament. Erasmus's edition is also noteworthy for the frequently controversial annotations he makes upon Biblical texts. He noted that mistranslations in the Vulgate had affected Catholic practice over the centuries, including the exhortation in Matthew 4:17, *'metanoeîte'*, which had been erroneously translated in the Latin as *'poenitentiam agite'* or 'do penance' when in fact it simply meant 'repent'. This nuance in meaning led many of the reformers to reject pious activities in favour of true conversion of the heart. Erasmus's quest for accuracy even led him to introduce paging in his New Testament. Previously, the recto side of leaves may have been numbered, but with the addition of page numbers on both sides of the leaf scholars and exegetes could allow for ever greater precision when doing textual comparison.

8   *Biblia Sacra, hebraice, chaldaice, græce et latine.* Antwerp: Christophe Plantin, 1569-1572.

In 1565 the great Humanist printer, Christophe Plantin, first conceived the idea of replacing Cardinal Ximénes de Cisneros's celebrated trilingual Bible that had appeared in 1517. Realizing that such an enterprise would also require a wealthy patron, he turned to King Philip II of Spain after deciding not to throw in his lot with Protestants in the wake of the Antwerp iconoclastic riots of 1566. This polyglot Bible, arguably Plantin's greatest typographical monument, was a collaborative effort from the start. It combined the linguistic and organizational skills of the orientalist Benito Arias Montano (1527-1598) with the talents of other Humanists like Andreas Masius (1514-1573), Guy Lefèvre de la Boderie (1541-1598), and Franciscus Raphelengius (1539-1597). The result was a new five-volume Bible in Hebrew, Greek, Latin, Syriac, and Chaldaic, accompanied by three additional volumes of reference materials, including grammars and dictionaries to assist in deciphering the ancient languages. The polyglot, however, was resisted in certain

quarters, especially Spain, where there was tremendous suspicion of the 'Judaizers', or those scholars who emphasized the necessity of returning to the original Hebrew sources in order to understand the nuances of Scripture better. Misgivings had also increased ever since the Council of Trent's 1546 decree reasserting the pre-eminence of the Vulgate text. Not surprisingly, papal approval was hesitant, but finally granted by Gregory XIII in 1572. Because this polyglot contained numerous errors, it was not a resounding success, and it was quickly superseded by other Biblical projects. Nevertheless, Plantin's polyglot, together with its accompanying apparatus of maps of the Holy Land, plans of ancient buildings, essays on numismatics, weights and measures, represents a significant milestone in the development of 'the modern knowledge industry'. Perhaps more importantly, polyglots such as this one forced scholars to look beyond Western Christendom when revising Biblical texts, especially for the production of vernacular editions.

English Bibles of the
Protestant Reformation

On 31 October 1517, when Martin Luther nailed his ninety-five theses to the door of the Castle Church in Wittenberg, he set in motion the Protestant Reformation. But the true reformation began in the mind and heart of this professor of Biblical literature as he poured over the Epistles of Paul and in particular Paul's thoughts about *solo fidei,* or 'salvation by faith alone', as expressed in the Epistle to the Romans. There has always been, in the life of the Church, an intimate and inseparable relationship between the study of the Bible and the birthing of reformation. In the period of the Protestant Reformation this was certainly true for Martin Luther, but also for John Calvin, John Knox and a multitude of other reformers. But the connection did not end in the sixteenth century.

The very same could be said of the Church in subsequent eras. In the eighteenth century the great spokespersons for the abolition of slavery, men such as John Newton and William Wilberforce, were students of the Bible who drew on the great Biblical themes of 'amazing grace' to make their impassioned appeals for reformation within their slave-based society. The impact of the Bible's constant call for reformation was no less apparent in the twentieth century. Great world leaders like Martin Luther King, Jr. and Ghandi based their doctrines of non-violent protest, and the equality and freedom of all peoples at least in part on their understanding of the Exodus story and their study of the life and ministry of Jesus as told in the Gospels.

Now, as Christianity moves into the twenty-first century, reformation is once more a theme as the ancient call of the Psalmist, to 'Sing to the Lord a new song; sing to the Lord, all the earth' stirs the Church to new forms and styles of engagement with the world, including contemporary worship and hymnody. Praise with trumpet, harp and lyre, tambourine and dancing, strings, flute and cymbals have found their way back into worship and it is a joy to behold.

Living Faith, a Statement of Christian Belief prepared recently by the Presbyterian Church in Canada, sums up the lively importance of the Bible as a reforming agent in the life of believers when it declares, 'The Church is in constant need of Reform because of the failure and sin which mark its life in every age. The Church is present when the Word is truly preached.' As the Church moves humbly and by constant reformation from 'seeing through a glass darkly', toward that day when, 'we shall see face to face' it will continue to be by virtue of Him whom Christians call the Living Word speaking through the written word, the Bible.

The Rev. Harvey Self, Moderator of the 135th General Assembly,
Presbyterian Church in Canada.

9   *The New Testament in English, Translated by John Wycliffe, circa* MCCCLXXX. London: Printed at Chiswick by C. Whittingham for W. Pickering, 1848.

In the 1380s, Middle English Bibles began to appear, whole or in parts, that were associated with the name of John Wycliffe, an Oxford scholar and priest known as 'the Morningstar of the Reformation'. It is perhaps more appropriate, however, to credit these Bibles to Wycliffe's followers, the Lollards who, like him, believed in the absolute supremacy of Scripture and the right of all Christians to interpret its words for themselves, a thesis that could threaten the authority of both Church and Crown. If Wycliffe himself were one of the translators, his contribution must have been confined to his latter days, though quite early in the translation process itself. These English manuscript Bibles contained no extraneous matter - only the Scriptural text was included, with very few glosses. The appearance of the so-called 'Wycliffe Bible' also coincides with the first official ecclesiastical censure of Biblical translation in England. Reacting to the allegedly heterodox teachings of Wycliffe and the Lollards, Archbishop Thomas Arundel forbade the translation of the Scriptures into English in the *Constitutiones* of 1409. Those who violated the law were subject to excommunication and, in some cases, death by burning. Pickering's 1848 edition purports to be a transcription of the earliest-known Wycliffite Bible, printed from a contemporary manuscript formerly in the monastery of Sion in Middlesex.

10 *The Newe Testament.* Antwerp: Martin de Keyser, 1534. (The Tyndale New Testament.)

Since making a vernacular translation of the Bible remained illegal in England at the beginning of the sixteenth century, those interested in undertaking such an enterprise either had to do their work in secret or emigrate. In 1525 William Tyndale, a Gloucestershire priest and humanist, moved to the relative safety of Cologne to translate his New Testament, but did not even complete the Gospel of Matthew before his work was suspended because of civil and religious unrest. It was not until the following year that he finished his work at Worms and six thousand copies were smuggled into England, costing intrepid readers the equivalent of one week's wages to purchase it. By all accounts, Tyndale was a skilled linguist; he studied Greek at Magdalen College, Oxford, and likely acquired his knowledge of Hebrew while in Germany. His New Testament was immediately denounced by the English bishops, not only because it was an illegal translation, but also because both King and hierarchy feared the unsettling influence of Lutheranism, especially as manifest in Tyndale's prologues to the Epistles which were based on Luther's originals. Of even greater concern was that ordinary laypersons, now capable of understanding Sacred Writ, might begin to interpret it for themselves. The contraband books were immediately ordered burnt by Archbishop William Warham (d. 1532) as soon as any appeared. Only one complete copy of the 1526 Testament survives, at the Stuttgart Landesbibliothek, with incomplete copies found at the British Library and St Paul's Cathedral. The copy on display was printed in 1534 and represents a careful revision of Tyndale's earlier work. Together with the other reformers of his day, Tyndale insisted that the Bible be translated into vernacular and released from the allegorical interpretations so common in the medieval church. Tyndale, therefore, asserted that the plain meaning of the Bible could only be understood in England in an English translation. As if such a radical idea were not enough, he also ran afoul of the King by denouncing his divorce from Catherine of Aragon. In 1535, he was arrested in Antwerp where he was working on a new translation of the Hebrew Scriptures. The following year he was strangled and burned at the stake near Brussels. Only days before his execution he wrote a letter to the prison warden saying, 'Most of all I earnestly entreat and implore you to ask the officer to allow me my Hebrew Bible, Hebrew Grammar and Hebrew Dictionary, so that I may spend my time in those studies.' Although all unapproved vernacular translations were opposed by the Church, no version was so violently suppressed as Tyndale's New Testament. All such efforts notwithstanding, ninety per cent of his translation survived into the Authorized Version of the Bible, licensed under King James I and still beloved by the English-speaking world.

11 *The Newe Testament both Latine and Englyshe ech Correspondent to the other after the Vulgare Texte, Communely called S. Jeroms.* Southwark: Printed by J. Nicolson, 1538. (The Coverdale New Testament.)

Tyndale's translation, though formally condemned by Church and State, served as the catalyst for the publication of the first legal version of the English Scriptures. Since the reading public had now acquired a taste for such forbidden fruit, the Convocation of Canterbury petitioned Henry VIII for an authorized vernacular translation in 1534. The project was undertaken by Miles Coverdale (1488-1568), a Cambridge graduate and priest. Coverdale was no linguist; in the dedicatory letter to his 1537 Bible he confesses that he did not know Hebrew and had but a passing

familiarity with Greek. Since he had relied on the Latin text as his primary source, rather than Hebrew or Greek manuscripts, his 1535 version was quickly judged inferior and regarded simply as a translation of a translation. Coverdale, however, did consult several contemporary sources for his edition including Tyndale, a new 1528 Latin translation of the Scriptures by the Italian Hebraist Sancte Pagnini, as well as Luther's German Bible. The dedicatory epistle to the King in this 1538 diglot explains why he decided to attempt yet another edition of the New Testament so soon after finishing his complete Bible. His intention was to assist the faithful at Mass since the readings were still being proclaimed in Latin as 'is costumably red in the church' even after Henry's secession from Rome. Coverdale's hope was 'that in co[m]parynge these two textes together, they maye the better understonde the one by ye other.' This Testament, printed with the Vulgate and English on facing pages, was so replete with errors that Coverdale repudiated it immediately and had a second edition printed under his supervision by François Regnault in Paris. As with several items on display in this exhibition, this copy was previously owned by the Toronto newspaper publisher and politician, John Ross Robertson (1841-1918).

12 *The Byble, whych is all the Holy Scripture: in whych are Contayned the Olde and Newe Testament, Truelye & Purely translated into Englishe.* London: Thomas Raynalde and William Hyll, 1549. (The Matthew Bible.)

Large portions of Coverdale's text migrated into a new Bible that appeared later in 1537 and came to be known as the 'Matthew Bible'. The translation was ascribed to one 'Thomas Matthew', a pseudonym for John Rogers, the first Marian martyr who would be executed in 1555. Rogers was in fact the editor; he drew upon Tyndale for the Pentateuch and historical books of the Old Testament, and Coverdale for the prophets. He was also influenced by the first French Protestant Bible printed at Neuchâtel in 1535, as well as a recent Latin version by Sancte Pagninus. Given the expense of the first printing (about £500) it is perhaps not surprising that the printer, Richard Grafton, requested that the chancellor, Thomas Cromwell, officially license his Bible as a protection against those who did not believe that the King was actually behind the project. Royal approval was obtained in August 1537, permitting the text to bear the inscription 'Set forth with the king's most gracious licence.' Some fifteen hundred copies were printed, and the book proved so popular that other printers began producing smaller inferior versions in minuscule print. It was disseminated in large numbers throughout the sixteenth century, even after the publication of the Great Bible. Several problems, however, attended this new version. The English Reformation was essentially conservative in nature, and a new translation of the Scriptures based on the work of continental reformers was immediately suspect. Particularly galling was the decision to arrange the Biblical books according to Luther's order, with those whose canonicity he questioned -

Hebrews, James, Jude, and Revelation - placed together at the end. The explanatory marginal notes added to this 1549 edition made a contentious book even more controversial. The last edition of the Matthew Bible appeared in 1551.

13   *The Byble in Englyshe.* Paris: François Regnault; London: Richard Grafton & Edward Whitchurch, 1539. (The Great Bible.)

In 1538, Thomas Cromwell, Chancellor of England, commanded that every parish church should have a large copy of the English Bible available for reading and consultation by the clergy and laity alike. The result was this massive tome, better known as 'The Great Bible'. The iconic title page to this, the only formally authorized copy of the English Scriptures in history, boasts that it was 'truly translated after the veryte of the Hebrue and Greke textes, by ye dylygent studye of Dyuerse excellent learned men, expert in the forsayde tonges'. The pride derived from this endeavour, however, is perhaps best expressed in the Holbeinesque woodcuts that adorn the title page, depicting Henry VIII distributing the English Bible to his enraptured subjects through the auspices of Archbishop Thomas Cranmer and the soon-to-be disgraced Cromwell. God himself appears stooped in a small cameo over the King's head, almost unnoticed. Coverdale was the scholar entrusted with the task of editing this 'new' version in a way that would be acceptable to the increasingly conservative tastes of the time. Thus, it is effectively a recension of John Roger's revision of Tyndale's original translation. The decision to have this Bible printed in France may seem odd, but was based on the fact that the production quality of Parisian books was far superior to those being printed in England at the time. It also reflects the reality that there were still many conservatives at home sufficiently opposed to the venture, especially within the episcopate, who would more than happily have disrupted its course. Work was in fact brought to a halt when the French Inquisitor General, Matthew Ory, issued an order against corrupt translations, and Coverdale and the printer Richard Grafton were

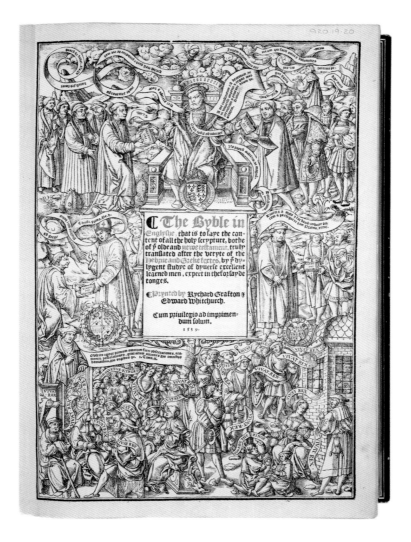

forced to flee to London with as many printed sheets as they could carry, to complete the project at home. A second, revised edition including Cranmer's preface appeared in April of 1540, with a sixth edition printed by November of 1541. It is worthy of note that while Cromwell's image remained on the title page, his coat of arms was expunged from the fourth edition of 1540, following his execution for, ironically, heresy.

14 *The First Tome or Volume of the Paraphrase of Erasmus vpon the Newe Testamente.* London: Edward Whitchurch, 1548, [i.e. 1549.]

Erasmus's desire to return to the linguistic sources of the Scriptures affected the broad spectrum of Christianity, from the most conservative Catholics to the most radical Protestants. His summaries and interpretations of the New Testament, for example, proved to be so popular among both Catholics and Protestants alike, that King Edward VI decreed that copies of his Paraphrases should be placed alongside the Great Bible in every parish church in England to guide the reader through the difficult passages. Edward's stepmother, Katherine Parr (1512-1548), and half-sister, the Princess Mary, both translated portions of the paraphrases into English themselves; it is, in fact, Mary's translation of the Gospel of John which appears here. England had lagged behind Germany and France in producing a vernacular edition of the Paraphrases until Miles Coverdale edited this first English version in 1548; he was personally responsible for the translation of the Epistles to the Romans, Corinthians, and Galatians. Since Erasmus did not write a paraphrase of Revelation, it was later supplied by the Swiss reformer, Leo Jud (1482-1542), and subsequently translated into English by Edward Allen.

15 *The Nevve Testament of Our Lord Iesus Christ: Conferred diligently with the Greke, and best approued Translations.* Geneva: Printed by Conrad Badius, 1557. (The Geneva New Testament.)

The Reformation was formally adopted at Geneva in May of 1536; shortly thereafter Jean Girard, a Protestant printer from the canton of Vaud arrived in the city at the invitation of Guillaume Farel, to take up his trade there. The city quickly saw success as a printing centre, not only because it had declared early for the Reformation, but also because of its geographical situation on the trade routes between the various well-established commercial book fairs. The 1550s witnessed a surge of Biblical translation in the city with the appearance of twenty-two editions of the French Protestant Bible as well as editions in both Greek and Latin. A little group of English Protestants, exiles from Queen Mary's England, became infected with this fervour and assumed the task of once again translating the New Testament into English. Presiding over the project was the English reformer and Biblical scholar William Whittingham (d. 1579). The result was a portable book that was largely derivative, and primarily based on Tyndale's earlier edition, though it was also influenced by Beza's new 1556 Latin translation. It was, however, the introduction of the distinctly Protestant interpretive marginal annotations which was to set this New Testament apart from its predecessors, and also establish it as the enemy of the conservative element within the English church. With its roman type, as well as chapter and verse divisions, its clarity of print, layout, and doctrine made it immediately popular with the Puritans who had survived the ravages of Mary's reign.

16   *The Bible and Holy Scriptures, Conteined in the Olde and Newe Testament.* Geneva: Rowland Hall, 1560. (The Geneva Bible.)

This Bible, commonly known as the 'Geneva' was the first complete English Bible printed in roman type. Like the New Testament that preceded it by three years, it was translated by a small group of Marian exiles living in Geneva, including Miles Coverdale and Thomas Gilby, working under the direction of William Whittingham. It is also noteworthy for being the first complete English Bible to feature chapter and verse divisions, chapter headings, as well as running titles. In short, it is this format of the Bible that established what the Scriptures would look like in the English-speaking world. The New Testament was thoroughly revised, and three editions would be printed at Geneva before the first London edition was printed by Christopher Barker in 1575. Four years later it became the official Bible of Scotland, when the Scots Parliament required every substantial householder to

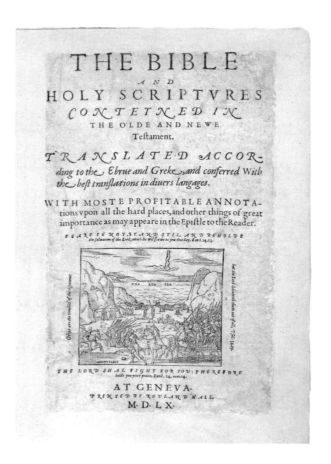

purchase a copy. While it never achieved that status in England, it was the *de facto* Bible of Elizabethan society. Its marginalia and explanatory notes were distinctly Calvinist in tone, thereby endearing it especially to the Puritans, but eventually setting it at odds with King James I. For three generations it maintained its supremacy as the Bible of the people with at least one hundred and forty editions appearing between 1560 and 1644; indeed, about a half a million Geneva Bibles were printed and sold between 1560 and 1620 alone. An examination of the King James Bible of 1611 shows that its translators were influenced more by the Geneva than by any other English version.

17 *The Holie Bible, Conteynyng the Olde Testament and the Newe.* London: Richard Jugge, 1568. (The Bishops' Bible.)

One reason to explain why the Geneva Bible did not find favour within certain segments of the English establishment was because it was fashioned beyond the control of the guardians of Anglican orthodoxy, namely the Church's bishops. To combat Geneva's influence, therefore, the Bishop of Ely, Richard Cox (d. 1581), suggested that a new translation be undertaken that would be acceptable to both the Catholic and Protestant wings of the Elizabethan church. This new version, which was first printed in 1568, came to be known as 'The Bishops' Bible' since it was translated by a group of scholars, several of them Hebraists, drawn from within the English episcopacy. Since the translators worked independently, the results were often uneven, and in some places, passages previously translated by Coverdale or the Geneva committee were merely duplicated. Archbishop Matthew Parker (1504-1575), who recommended the project to Queen Elizabeth, insisted that all 'bitter notis uppon any text' be eliminated, and that the translation follow the Great Bible as closely as possible, except in those places where it could be demonstrated that the wording had clearly departed in meaning from the original Hebrew and Greek. Despite Parker's admonition concerning marginalia, explanatory notes with a strikingly Calvinist tone did make their way into the text, and are particularly evident in the Epistle to the Romans. Even more forthright notes, some copied directly from Tyndale, may be found in the subsequent editions of the Bishops' Bible from 1573, 1576 and 1608. With the accession of the high churchman John Whitgift (d. 1604) as Archbishop of Canterbury in 1583, the battle against the Geneva Bible was resumed in earnest. One of his first orders was that the Bishop's Bible alone should be used in public worship. As a result, it is estimated that some three hundred thousand copies were printed to serve a population of around four and a half million people.

18 *The Bible: Translated according to the Ebrew and Greeke, and Conferred with the Best Translations in Divers Languages.* London: Christopher Barker, 1580. (The Geneva Bible.)

This copy of the Geneva Bible is interesting simply because it is printed in 'black letter' or gothic type, which would appear to be a regressive choice. Genevan printers had been producing Latin Bibles in roman rather than 'black letter' since 1534; yet after almost twenty years of providing a Bible in simple, easy-to-read roman type, English Geneva Bibles began to appear in this 'new' format in 1579.

There is no surviving explanation for this apparently retrograde decision, other than the suggestion that it may have reflected popular and traditional expectations of what the Sacred Word should look like. The fact that the rival Bishops' Bible was also printed in black letter may help to account for the reversal. Besides the type, the major difference with the black letter editions was the omission of all maps and illustrations. They did, however, contain 'The Summe of the Whole Scripture' and 'Questions and Answers on the Doctrine of Predestination and the Use of God's Word and Sacraments', both placed before the New Testament. In addition, the original tables found at the end of the 1560 edition were replaced with much longer works entitled 'Two Profitable and Fruitful Concordances, or Tables Large and Alphabeticall' written by Robert F. Herrey. It is worthy of note that it was the Geneva black letter quarto of 1592 that was carried by the Pilgrims to America on the *Mayflower* in 1620.

19   *The Bible: that is, the Holy Scriptures Conteined in the Olde and Newe Testament.* London: Christopher Barker, 1587. (The Geneva Bible.)

This copy of the Geneva Bible was the first to include Laurence Tomson's enormously influential English translation of Theodore Beza's Latin New Testament of 1565. Tomson (1539-1608), linguist and scholar, had been the personal secretary to Sir Francis Walsingham, Secretary of State to Queen Elizabeth I, and may have known Beza personally from his own diplomatic travels. He first published his New Testament independently in 1576, with marginalia far more extensive than those found in the original Geneva version. Wherever Tomson supplements Beza's own comments, which he frequently does, the text is printed in a neat italic. Interestingly, the only book which fails to have significant marginal notes is Revelation, perhaps reflecting Tomson's more cautious, diplomatic nature when approaching a Book so intimately associated with cataclysm and the Pope as antichrist, as it was in earlier editions of the Geneva version. It would not be until

1599 that Revelation received the full treatment, diatribes and all, when the notes of Franciscus Junius (1545-1602), a survivor of the French Wars of Religion, were added to the text.

20 *The Bible, that is, The Holy Scriptures, Conteined in the Old and New Testament.*
London: Robert Barker, 1610. (The Geneva Bible.)

Despite the publication date on its title page, this Bible was actually printed in 1611 (as stated in its colophon), the same year in which the first edition of the King James Bible appeared. The Puritan faction was suspicious of the new royally sanctioned text precisely because it might displace the influence of their venerable Geneva Bible, so beloved by Calvinists within the Church of England. The King's decision to omit the explanatory notes, perhaps the most prominent feature of the Geneva version, from his new Bible was particularly galling. Reflecting some thirty years later on the publication of the rival version, the church historian Thomas Fuller (1608-1661) wrote that 'some of the Brethren ... complained that they could not see into the sense of the Scripture for lack of the spectacles of those Geneva Annotations.' Ironically, in order to placate the more Protestant wing of the church, the King James Bible was occasionally printed with Geneva's marginal notes from 1642 until well into the eighteenth century. In 1644, the last Geneva Bible was printed at Amsterdam, only after which did the King James Version begin to achieve its iconic status.

Bibles from the English Roman Catholic Tradition

When Catholic bishops prepared the document on Divine Revelation at the Second Vatican Council (1962-1965), they entitled it *Dei verbum,* 'The Word of God'. In the first place, this refers to Jesus as 'Word of God' who Christians believe 'became flesh and dwelt among us'. But *Dei verbum* also speaks of the revelation of God which became flesh in human language - in what we normally call 'the Word of God', or the Bible.

Christians treasure their encounters with the Word through the experience of life, prayer, and especially through the Sacraments and written texts that they believe are inspired by the Holy Spirit. Over the first few centuries of its existence, the young Church discerned which of those early writings, from both before and after the coming of Christ, should be considered inspired by God, and passed them on as the Biblical Word.

The work of many medieval monks, who adopted 'To pray and work' as their motto, was copying and illuminating Biblical texts. Later Gutenberg and others made the transition from manuscript to the printed page. In the wake of the doctrinal disputes of the Reformation, the Catholic Church became concerned about the principle of the 'Bible alone', asserting instead that the written text is best interpreted within the context of the faith community. To serve that community in England, the missionary priests of Rheims prepared a Roman Catholic English translation in the late sixteenth century.

In the twentieth century, the encyclical letter *Divino Afflante Spiritu* (1943) of Pope Pius XII (1876-1958), and especially Vatican II's *Dei verbum* (1965), have led Catholic Christians to study and to pray the Biblical text with renewed attentiveness, interpreting it within the context of both academic scholarship and the living faith of the community of disciples where we believe the Lord continues to come among us in Word and Sacrament.

Many now encounter the Divine in the Biblical text through an ancient prayer tradition known as *'Lectio Divina'*, or 'Sacred Reading'. After an introductory period of prayer modeled on the call of Samuel, 'Speak, Lord, your servant is listening', a small portion of Scripture is read, often aloud. It is then reread, verse by verse, with a time of prayerful reflection between each verse. A common approach is to ask oneself: what does this text say to my head, my heart, and my hands? How does it lead me to know, to love, and to serve God, through adoration and through the practical service of my neighbour?

The Most Reverend Thomas C. Collins,
Roman Catholic Archbishop of Toronto

21 *The New Testament of Jesus Christ.* Rheims: John Fogny, 1582. (The Rheims New Testament.)

At the Council of Trent, it became a matter of heated debate whether the translation of the Bible into the vernacular would be to the benefit or detriment of the Roman Church in the wake of the Protestant Reformation. Bishops on both sides of the divide argued passionately. The 1546 Decree of the Council of Trent, *Insuper,* officially designated the Latin Vulgate to be the Bible of Catholicism, and therefore the only version permitted for public reading, preaching, and exposition. A further papal edict issued in 1559 also sided with the conservatives and formally forbade translation into the modern languages. Given such restrictions, it is remarkable that a Catholic version of the Scriptures appeared in English less than twenty-five years later. In reality, its publication is a reflection of the desperation felt by exiled English Catholics who recognized that their co-religionists at home would not long be able to withstand the lure of popular, easily accessible versions of the English Protestant Bible, particularly the Geneva. Because they had been

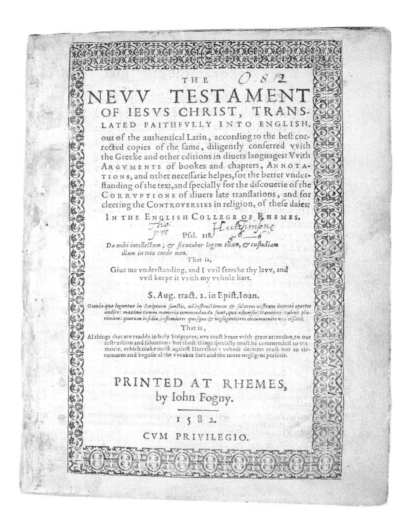

persecuted for the practice of their faith at home, the English Catholics established a seminary at Douai, France in 1568, from which they were evicted for political reasons in 1578. The seminary was re-established at Rheims later the same year, around the time that Father Gregory Martin (d. 1582), former Fellow of St John's College, Oxford, a Greek and Hebrew scholar, began his translation of the Latin Vulgate Bible into English. In 1580, the seminary rector William Allen (1532-1594) successfully petitioned Pope Gregory XIII (1502-1585) to grant a dispensation to

53

allow the work to proceed to print in order to combat the influence of Protestantism at home. Martin worked diligently at the project, translating two chapters each day, with the assistance of several other clerics, including Richard Bristow (1538-1581), Thomas Worthington (1549-1627), and William Reynolds (1544-1594). Martin died of consumption shortly after completing the project. Because this version was a translation of a translation, it was considered an inferior product by those who had worked directly with the Greek *Urtext.* The initial print run of Rheims was massive: five thousand copies were printed and exported to England as contraband, enraging Queen Elizabeth and her counselors.

22 *The Holie Bible, Faithfully Translated into English, out of the Authentical Latin. Diligently Conferred with the Hebrew, Greeke, and other Editions in Diuers Languages.* Douai: Laurence Kellam, 1609-10. (The Douai-Rheims Bible.)

Although Gregory Martin had translated both the Hebrew and the Christian Scriptures before his death in 1582, the financially beleaguered community of exiled English Catholics was prevented from publishing a complete Bible until 1609, some twenty-seven years after the first appearance of the Rheims New Testament. By this time, the seminary had returned to its original home at Douai where this book was produced. As the subtitle notes, the volume includes 'arguments of the bookes, and chapters, annotations, tables, and other helpes, for better understanding of the text, for discouerie of corruptions in some late translations, and for clearing controversies in religion'. It was the inclusion of marginalia, similar in their polemical style if not content to the Geneva Bible, which likely made the translation acceptable to Roman authorities, since such notes explained to readers the Catholic sense in which the Scriptures were to be understood. Thus, the threat of personal interpretation, so contrary to established Catholic discipline, could largely be avoided. The translation had its problems, however, not the least of which was stylistic. In places, Martin appears to have bor-

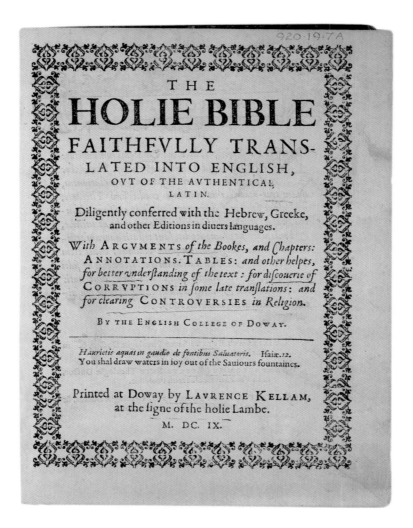

rowed some elegant phrases directly from the Coverdale and Geneva versions; but since the translators had to be slavishly faithful to the 1547 Louvain edition of the Latin Vulgate, the phraseology tended to be stilted, causing even Catholic prelates of later centuries to find fault. Instead of beginning with 'The Lord is my shepherd, I shall not want', the Douai-Rheims twenty-third Psalm reads 'Our Lord ruleth me, and nothing shal be wanting to me'. Francis Kenrick (1797-1863), Archbishop of Baltimore, complained that 'scrupulous adherence of the translators to the letter of the Vulgate in rendering the names of places and persons, and their desire to retain Hebrew and Greek words, which had been preserved in the Latin, and their study to express the Latin words by corresponding English terms of Latin origin, rather than to draw "from the wells of English undefiled," detracted much from the perspicuity and beauty of their version.'

23   *The Text of the New Testament of Jesus Christ, translated out of the vulgar Latine by the Papists of the Traiterous Seminarie at Rhemes.* London: Thomas Adams, 1617.

The Puritan minister and scholar, William Fulke (1536-1589), was responsible for this contentious text in which he attacked not only the Rheims translation of the Scriptures, but Catholic doctrine in general. As the subtitle explains, he accomplished his task 'with arguments of bookes, chapters, and annotations, pretending to discouer the corruptions of diuers translations and to cleare the controuersies of these days.' It had been Fulke's practice, especially towards the end of his life, to enter into public disputations with Catholic recusants, the most famous of which involved the Jesuit, Edmund Campion (1540-1581) shortly before his execution. This book, originally printed in 1589, displays the Rheims text parallel to the Bishops' Bible, with Fulke's polemical commentary at the end of each chapter. Fulke was also responsible for a diatribe against the contemporary Catholic philosophy of Biblical translation in *A Defense of the Sincere and True Translation of the Holy Scriptures into the English Tongue* (1583) which, together with this book, exerted significant influence over the translators of King James's Bible, as did Fulke's thesis that every work of translation is also a work of interpretation. Ironically, it was through this parallel presentation of the Catholic and Protestant versions of the Scriptures that King James's translators may have first encountered the forbidden Rheims edition, and incorporated some of its finer details into their final product.

24 *The Holy Bible faithfully translated into English out of the authentical Latin, dili-*
gently conferred with the Hebrew, Greek, & other Editions in diuers Languages.
Rouen: John Cousturier, 1635. (Douai-Rheims Bible.)

The second edition of the Douai-Rheims Old Testament first appeared as
volume one of this two-volume set, together with a commentary, marginalia, and
instructive tables, all directed towards the 'discouerie of corruptions in some late

translations, and for clearing controuersies in religion'. The paper, type, and woodcuts were all considered somewhat inferior to the first printing of 1609-1610. Although Protestant versions had long included beautifully engraved title pages similar in style to the one found in this edition, Puritans were becoming particularly offended by the depiction of the prophets and evangelists which, they claimed, turned the book into an icon. Their concerns forced English printers to reconsider the inclusion of illustrations of any kind in future Protestant Bibles since they might give the impression that their editions were no better than 'popish entertainments'. It would be one hundred years after this publication before another complete Catholic Bible was reprinted. In 1692, the Fisher copy was in the possession of Gervas Hamond, a recusant Catholic who was reported to the Leeds Session in August 1691 as living at Towton with his wife Katherine. He also refused to take the oath of fidelity to King George I in 1715 after the Northern Insurrection.

25   *The New Testament of Jesus Christ.* London? 1738. (Rheims New Testament.)

This fifth edition of the Rheims New Testament represents its first independent reprinting since 1633 and its first appearance in folio. The omission of both the place of publication as well as the printer from the title page may perhaps be owing to the dangers still implicit in the production of a Catholic version of the Scriptures prior to Catholic emancipation which did not seriously begin until the end of the eighteenth century. While some scholars believe London to be its place of origin, others propose Douai, where one of its suggested revisers, Bishop Richard Challoner (1691-1781), had been a student. Beautifully executed in a fine, crisp type, this edition includes an engraved title page and portraits of the evangelists. The various linguistic and stylistic defects of the Douai-Rheims Bible had long been recognized by English-speaking Catholics. As a result Cornelius Nary (1660-1738), an Irish priest, published a revised version in London in 1709, which was republished in Paris in 1717. One of the Douai seminary priests, Robert Witham (1715-1738), published another revision in 1736 'with learned notes, void of acrimony', to which Bishop Challoner gave his approbation. Other revised editions appeared in 1788 and 1789 - the last two printed at Liverpool.

26   *The Holy Bible Translated from the Latin Vulgat.* Dublin? 1749-1750. (Challoner Bible.)

Perhaps as a result of his involvement with the work of earlier revisers, Challoner came to recognize that the Douai-Rheims Bible, even with minor adjustments, was no longer serving the needs of the Catholic faithful, especially the poor. He, therefore, published his own thoroughly revised version in five portable volumes, 'with notes, few in number and of a mild character.' Richard Challoner, titular Bishop of Debra and latterly Vicar Apostolic of the London District, was a convert to Roman Catholicism and is credited with responsibility for the modern Douai-Rheims version of the Bible. In the process of his revision he modernized the spelling, abolished many of its Latinisms, and altered the text significantly - so much so that, according to both John Henry Cardinal Newman (1801-1890) and Nicholas Cardinal Wiseman (1802-1865), this text should not be considered merely a revision of an old standard, but should be received as a new translation altogether. By his hand, for example, 'Azymes' becomes 'unleavened bread'; Christ has now 'emptied' rather than 'exinanited himself'; and the 'scenopegia' is the 'feast of tabernacles'. Perhaps not surprisingly for a convert raised on the King James Bible, Challoner's style, with its flowing cadences, approaches more nearly the Protestant edition in both vocabulary and rhythm. His New Testament appeared in 1749, with the Old Testament printed the following year. A popular translation with the Catholic population, the second edition of the New Testament appeared almost immediately in 1750 with further editions in 1752, 1764, 1772, 1777, and 1792. Complete copies of the entire Scriptures were printed in 1794, 1796-1797, 1805, 1808, and 1811. The work was nevertheless not without its critics, and saw subsequent revisions throughout the nineteenth century. As Bishop Kenrick notes, Challoner was accused of having 'weakened considerably the style, by avoiding inversion, which often gives prominence to the subject of the sentence, and by inserting unnecessarily qualifying particles: but his revision was nevertheless favorably received, and has ever since been the standard of the many editions published in England, Ireland, Scotland, and the United States'. Fisher's copy was previously owned by Joseph B. Lightfoot (1828-1889), Bishop of Durham and a member of the Committee for the Revision of the Authorized Version of the New Testament.

27 *The Holy Bible Translated from the Latin Vulgate.* Manchester: Thomas Haydock, 1812-1814. (Haydock Bible.)

This popular folio edition of the Douai-Rheims was actually a revision of Challoner's Bible. Edited by Father George Haydock (1774-1849), it restored many of the more polemical annotations found in earlier versions of the Douai-Rheims Bible, as well as notes by Don Augustin Calmet (1672-1757), Willem Hessels van Est (1542-1613) and other Catholic scholars. A system of abbreviations was implemented indicating which notes were original and which had been added by later commentators. Issued in separate numbers, the first sheets of the Old Testament appeared on 11 July 1811, and subsequent issues appeared every two weeks at the cost of one shilling each. The initial run was fifteen hundred copies, but the popularity of the publication soon forced a second edition. The Bible would be republished five times before 1853, and was considered the standard Catholic translation throughout the English-speaking world for several generations. In 1961, the Haydock Bible enjoyed a brief return to prominence when President John F. Kennedy took his oath of office with his left hand resting on one. It was not without its contemporary critics, however, in Catholic and Protestant academic circles. The pre-eminent Anglican expert on Biblical

editions, Canon Henry Cotton (1790-1879) noted, for example, that while Haydock was 'pious and warm-hearted' he was not possessed of 'high scholarship'; he also criticized him for his injudicious selection of annotations done, he felt, merely to keep the presses rolling even when the notes bore no relation to the text at hand. The Haydock brothers, George and Thomas, had been educated at Douai, fleeing the Seminary there during the course of the French Revolution. While George continued on to ordination, Thomas established relatively unsuccessful Catholic publishing houses in Manchester and Dublin.

61

28 *A New Version of the Four Gospels: With Notes Critical and Explanatory.* London: Joseph Booker, 1836.

This new translation of the Gospels was the work of the historian, Father John Lingard (1771-1851), who used both the Vulgate and ancient Syriac versions of the New Testament as his points of departure. Published anonymously by 'a Catholic', the translation was hailed not only as new, but also elegant with very few but useful notes. Bishop Kenrick acknowledged Lingard as the guide in his own work of Biblical translation, eventually culminating in the publication of the Gospels in 1849 and a complete New Testament in 1851. Lingard, who like the Haydock brothers had fled Douai in the wake of the French revolutionary army, was a progressive in his pastoral practice, insisting that the liturgy be simple and intelligible to both his parishioners and Protestant visitors alike. To that end, for example, he insisted that the Passion be declaimed in English during Holy Week services while he quietly read it in Latin as required. Better known for his *History of England* (1819-1830), he was an associate of the Royal Society of Literature, and in 1839 was elected to the Académie française. Lingard's *Gospels* was republished in 1851.

29 *The Four Gospels Translated from the Latin Vulgate and Diligently Compared with the original Greek Text, being a Revision of the Rhemish translation, with notes, critical and explanatory by Francis Patrick Kenrick.* New York: Edward Dungan & Brothers, 1849.

Francis Kenrick was born in Dublin, Ireland in 1796 and was ordained priest at the age of twenty-four. His career in the Church may best be described as meteoric, having been appointed coadjutor Bishop of Philadelphia in 1830 at the tender age of thirty-three, and Archbishop of Baltimore at fifty-four. Kenrick had displayed his acute scholarly abilities while still a seminarian at the Propaganda Fide College in Rome where he pursued his studies of the ancient Biblical languages as well as the standard courses in theology. It was while serving as Bishop of Philadelphia that he began his 'revision' of the Douai-Rheims Bible which he issued in six volumes between 1849 and 1860. *The Four Gospels* was the first to appear in the series and was largely intended as a vindication of the Vulgate from whose purity, he believed, the Greeks and Protestants had departed. Although somewhat suspicious of the historical-critical method emerging on the Continent, he nevertheless applied its principles by consulting Greek manuscripts when confronted by contentious New Testament expressions. He translated Matthew 3:2, *pœnitentiam agite*, for example, as 'repent' which, while consistent with the original Greek, ran contrary to the accepted Catholic rendering of 'do penance'. His translation was a resounding success in American Catholic circles, however, with the philosopher Orestes Brownson (1803-1876) declaring it 'the most important contribution to the branch of Catholic literature to which it pertains, that has recently, or to our knowledge ever, been made in the English language'. The Second Plenary Council of the bishops of the United States, meeting in 1866, declined to give it official status though it was highly regarded among Catholics until the end of the nineteenth century.

On loan from the John W. Graham Library, University of Trinity College

30   *The New Testament of Our Lord and Saviour Jesus Christ: Newly Translated from the Vulgate Latin at the Request of their Lordships, the Archbishops and Bishops of England and Wales.* New York: Sheed & Ward, 1944. (Knox New Testament.)

Like all Roman Catholic translations of the Scriptures done after the Council of Trent, this version of the New Testament, translated by Monsignor Ronald Knox (1888-1957), a convert from Anglicanism, was based on the Latin text, with one eye trained on the Greek originals. Knox doggedly followed the official Clementine Vulgate of 1592, even though he knew that it contained numerous corruptions. He justified his decision to incorporate the errors into his new English text, stating that 'that is how the thing stands in every Vulgate in the world nowadays, and it is no part of the translator's business to alter, on however good grounds, his original'. What Knox's version lacked in accuracy, however, it somewhat made up for in exquisite prose, since he was an acknowledged stylistic master. The page layout of his New Testament is modern inasmuch as Knox chose to use long lines arranged into paragraphs for the text, as one would find in a novel, rather than the traditional columns. In 1949 Knox published his translation of the Old Testament as well, again basing his work on the Vulgate. His Psalter, however, was translated from a new Roman edition which in turn had been translated directly from the ancient Hebrew. Together with the Douai-Rheims, the Knox version was the only other edition of the Bible authorized for the use of English Catholics before Pope Pius XII's revolutionary encyclical *Divino Afflante Spiritu* of 1943 encouraged Catholic translators to return to the original Hebrew and Greek sources of the Scriptures.

31   *The Jerusalem Bible.* Garden City: Doubleday, 1966.

A revolution in Roman Catholic Biblical scholarship occurred in 1943 when Pius XII freed exegetes from the bonds imposed by the Council of Trent which had allowed only the use of the Latin Vulgate in translation and teaching. The encyclical *Divino Afflante Spiritu* of 1943 insisted that Catholics return to the linguistic sources of the Scriptures, stating that 'there are now such abundant aids to the study of these languages that the Biblical scholar, who by neglecting them would deprive himself of access to the original texts, could in no wise escape the stigma of levity and sloth'. The *École biblique et archéologique française de Jérusalem*, administered by the Dominican Fathers, was one of the first Catholic institutions to seize this new opportunity, producing *Le Bible de Jérusalem* in parts from 1948 onwards. Under the direction of Father Alexander Jones, an English version was prepared in 1966. Twenty-seven collaborators assisted in the project which, while popular, garnered mixed reviews with criticism largely focusing on the process itself. After a passage of the Biblical text had been translated from the ancient languages into English, the wording was then compared with the French text. If necessary, it was then modified to ensure that there would be no logical departures from the original French introduction and extensive marginalia, which had already been translated directly from the French into English. In addition, others have criticized this version since it verges on paraphrase, attempting to communicate more the sense of the text rather than reproducing the syntactical and grammatical structure of the original. For all of its shortcomings, however, as a translation from the original Biblical languages, the *Jerusalem Bible* marks a milestone of serious English Catholic scholarship.

King James and his Bibles

In his vividly written masterpiece, *God's Secretaries,* Adam Nicolson tells us that King James's translators designed his Bible to be read in public worship. Before final approval, he says that they actually read it aloud to each other, listening for what T.S. Eliot later called 'the auditory imagination', that 'feeling for syllable and rhythm, penetrating far below the conscious levels of thought and feeling'.

Try it yourself with Proverbs 3:17. Say it aloud: 'Her ways are ways of pleasantness, and all her paths are peace'. You can conduct that rhythm, like music. Now read the 1961 New English Bible version: 'Her ways are pleasant ways, and all her paths lead to prosperity'. It's school-perfect - even reaching back for a good word from a KJV precursor, the Geneva Bible of 1560 - but it doesn't sing.

The old translation lodges itself deeply beneath conscious thought. Invite a random funeral gathering, a very ill person, or anyone in a hard place, to join in the recitation of the Lord's Prayer or the Twenty-third Psalm. The words of the King James still spill out, sometimes with tears. 'Deliver us from evil' - not 'the evil one'. 'Yea, though I walk through the valley of the shadow of death' - rather than 'a valley dark as death'. 'I will dwell in the house of the Lord forever' - not 'my whole life long' as the New English Bible would have it in each case.

That may not happen fifty years from now. Few children any longer learn anything 'by heart'; their memory halls are left unfurnished. Today's church attenders, instead of listening to Scripture clearly voiced, often follow indifferent readers on printed bulletins where words of power lie flattened and tamed, with little chance to seep soul-deep.

Of course, for study and understanding, new versions and paraphrases are essential, with their access to early manuscripts, and up-to-date English. 'The greatest of these is charity', as the King James Version would have it, no longer expresses what Paul meant to say.

In public worship, however, I prefer the New Revised Standard Version (1989). That's because, as its preface promises, it continues in 'the tradition of the King James Version', with only 'such changes as are warranted on the basis of accuracy, clarity, euphony, and current English usage'.

Euphony above all, as the Translators knew in 1611 - heart-deep music that sings the words of life.

The Very Rev. Bruce McLeod,
Moderator of the United Church of Canada, 1972-1974.

32 *The Holy Bible, Conteyning the Old Testament, and the New: Newly Translated out of the Originall Tongues: & with the Former Translations diligently Compared and Reuised, by His Maiesties speciall Co[m]mandement: Appointed to be read in Churches.* London: Robert Barker, 1611.

The King James Bible, first printed in 1611, had its roots in the tensions that existed in England between Anglicans and Puritans at the death of Queen Elizabeth I in 1603. Her successor, James VI of Scotland (1566-1625), was something of an unknown quantity south of the border. Puritans hoped that his Presbyterian upbringing would predispose him to favour their cause; Anglicans trusted that his belief in the divine right of Kings, as expressed in his recently published book *Basilikon Doron* or *The Kingly Gift,* might be exploited to support their ecclesiology. In the end, it was the Anglican preachers, particularly Richard Bancroft (1544-1610), Lancelot Andrewes (1555-1626), and John King (d. 1621), who persuaded the King that the security of his throne rested in the Church of England and its episcopal structure. Nevertheless, James, recognizing the fractious religious character of the kingdom he had inherited, summoned a conference to be held at Hampton Court in January of 1604, at which he hoped to resolve the religious differences between Anglicans and Puritans once and for all.

It was the Puritans, however, who left the Conference embarrassed and chastised by a King who was considered as able a theological disputant as any man in Europe. He afterwards wrote to Henry Howard, Earl of Northampton (1540-1614), saying 'They fledde me so from argument to argument, without ever ansouring me directlie, *ut est eorum moris,* as I was forced at last to saye unto thaime, that if any of thaime hadde bene in a colledge disputing with thair skollairs, if any of thaire disciples hadde ansourid thaim in that sorte, they wolde have fetchid him up in a place of replye & so shoulde the rodde have plyed upon the poor boyes buttokis'. The request for a new translation of the Bible was almost an afterthought, suggested by the Puritan divine, John Reynolds (1549-1607), who asked for a single, authorized text to replace the multiplicity of often errant versions still in circulation and in use in churches and homes throughout the country. To the amazement of the bishops, James agreed.

Behind the King's acquiescence, however, was his great antipathy towards the extraordinarily popular Geneva version, and in particular its marginalia. Although he claimed not to have known the Geneva Bible until coming to England in 1603, the fact is that it was the text, which had been declared the authorized Scottish version in 1579, on which he had been reared. His lack of regard for the translation seems to be implicit in his request made to the General Assembly of the Kirk to provide a new version of the Scriptures for Scottish use in 1601. By the time of the Hampton Court Conference, James had clearly come to associate English Puritans - and their Geneva Bible - with the Scottish Presbyterians, calling them 'brain sick and heady preachers'. Writing towards the end of his life, the Anglican controversialist Peter Heylyn (1599-1662) observed that 'that learned King hath told us in the Conference at Hampton-Court, that the Notes on the Genevan Bible were partial, untrue, seditious, and favouring too much of dangerous and trayterous conceits. For proof whereof he instanced in the Note of Exxod. 1. ver. 19 where they allow of disobedience unto Kings and Soveraign Princes: And secondly, in that on 2 Chron. 8.15,16. where Asa is taxed for not putting his Mother to death, but deposing her onely from the Regency, which before she executed. Of which last note the Scotish Presbyterians made especial use, not

only in deposing Mary their lawful Queen but prosecuting her openly and under hand till they had took away her life.'

A committee of translators was struck, divided into six 'companies', operating under rules established by Richard Bancroft, Bishop of London. The Bishops' Bible was to be followed as closely as possible, with the maintenance of the accepted ecclesiastical language. Perhaps most importantly, marginal notes were to be omitted, except where necessary to explain a Hebrew or Greek word. Each member of a given company was to take the same passage and translate from the original tongue into English. The text was then to be circulated among the other company men, resolving whatever differences may have arisen in the process. Having arrived at an agreed text, the company then would send the translation to the rest of the Committee before forwarding it to the King for his approval. Persistent disagreements were to be resolved by a meeting of the chief representatives of each company at the end of the process. Besides the Bishops' Bible, the other English versions which were to be consulted included Tyndale, the Matthew Bible, Coverdale, the Great Bible, and Geneva, copies of which were made available by the King's Printer, Robert Barker.

One company, under the direction of Lancelot Andrewes, Dean of Westminster, was charged with the translation of the books of the Old Testament from Genesis to the second Book of Kings; another, with William Barlow (d. 1613), Dean of Chester, at the head, assumed responsibility for the New Testament epistles. Two companies each from Oxford and Cambridge, under the chairmanship of the respective King's Professors for Hebrew and Greek, were responsible for the rest of the Scriptures, including the Apocrypha. In the end, some forty-seven accomplished translators were assembled from across England to undertake this mammoth work which finally saw the light of day in 1611. Ironically, in the preface entitled 'The Translators to the Reader', Biblical citations were always drawn from the Geneva Bible, not the new King James.

The book itself is equal in size and weight to the Bishops' Bible which it would eventually replace for liturgical use. It is difficult to say what exactly constitutes a true 'first edition' however, since the book actually came off the presses in two slightly different forms. The most notable variant is to be found at Ruth 3:15. One printing reads 'He went into the city' while the other reads 'She went into the city'. The Fisher copy is a so-called 'He' Bible, and is generally acknowledged to have the priority of issue. Modern King James' versions follow the 'She' Bible.

Although commonly known as the 'Authorized Version', this designation is something of a misnomer. While the King gave his approbation to the translation and permitted its use in public, he never insisted that it be the only copy of the Scriptures read in England, as was the case previously with the Great Bible. In some ways the King James Version assumed its authoritative status when its words were incorporated into the definitive 1662 revision of the Book of Common Prayer (with the exception of the Psalms, which remained in Coverdale's language). Although it was rejected by many within the Puritan party, owing to the omission of marginal notes, others objected to the use of gothic or black letter, which seemed regressive after several decades' use of clear, roman type. Nevertheless, the authority of this text is at least partially derived from its rhythm and words as they have seeped into the consciousness of English speakers the world over.

33 *The Holy Bible, Containing the Old Testament and the New.* London: Robert Barker, 1631.

It has been estimated that in the 250 years following the first printing of the King James Bible some fifteen hundred errors had crept into the text. This 1631 printing, popularly known as *The Wicked Bible*, is a perfect example of a cleric's worst fears surrounding translation. It derives its nickname from the rendering of Exodus 20:14

where the word 'not' has been omitted from the passage so that it reads, 'Thou shalt commit adultery'. In his *Cyprianus Anglicus* describing the life of Archbishop Laud, Peter Heylyn writes that 'His Majesty being made acquainted with [the error] by the Bishop of London, Order was given for calling the Printers into the High-Commission, where upon Evidence of the Fact, the whole Impression was called in, and the Printers deeply fined, as they justly merited.' The King's Printer, Robert Barker and his associates were fined the enormous sum of £300 for their offence, although it remains possible that the error was intentionally caused. Having the licence to print Bibles in the seventeenth century was essentially a licence to print money, so great was the demand for the book. It is now believed that a partisan of one of Barker's professional enemies, the rival printer, Bonham Norton (1565-1635) was responsible for infiltrating his establishment and causing the crisis. Some one thousand copies were printed before the order for their destruction was issued - an order that was so vigorously enforced that this edition of the Bible is among the rarest in the world. Barker died in 1643, a man broken in reputation and wealth.

34 *The Holy Bible, Containing ye Old and New Testaments. Newly Translated out of ye Originall Tongues, and with the Former Translations Diligently Compared and Revised.* London: John Field, Printer to the Parliament, 1653.

English culture in the seventeenth century was a study in contrasts, but its religious ethos was quintessentially Biblical. While there were some radical Protestants who had decided that the spiritually enlightened conscience superseded the need for the Scriptures, the majority were busy committing large portions of it to memory. One need only read the letters and addresses of Oliver Cromwell (1599-1658) to see that citations from Scripture are naturally woven into the fabric of speech and text, the references clearly recognizable to his intended audience. This portable copy of the Bible, with its inherent problems, is typical of Bibles printed

at this time. Demand increased rapidly, the result being that the books themselves were often shoddily produced and poorly edited with frequent printing errors. The privations of the English Civil War (1641-1651), the Commonwealth (1649-1653), and the Protectorate (1653-1659) only exacerbated the problem; with supplies running short, it often was necessary to print the text cheaply on the continent, especially in the Netherlands. This 1653 miniature Bible is essentially faithful to the revisions of 1638 with one very noteworthy error: in some early printing states I Corinthians 6:9 can read, 'Know ye not that the unrighteous shall inherit the kingdom of God?' turning the Apostle's message somewhat on its head.

35   *The Holy Bible: Containing the Old Testament and the New. Newly Translated Out of the Original Tongues, and with the Former Translations Diligently Compared and Revised, by His Majesties Speciall Command. Appointed to be Read in Churches.* Cambridge: Printed by John Field, 1668.

Civil unrest affected not only the social and political life of the nation in the middle of the seventeenth century, but also its print industry. After some years of confusion concerning who had the right to print the Bible, Oliver Cromwell

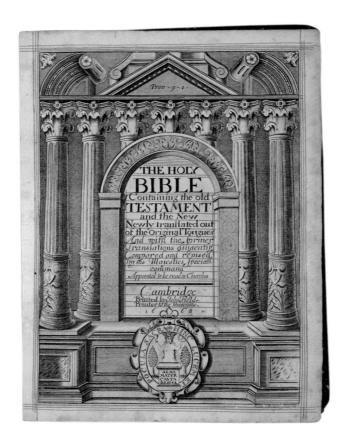

assigned that privilege to the partnership of Henry Hills and John Field in 1656. Field was also appointed printer to Cambridge University with a monopoly over the printing of the King James Bible. He managed to survive his close association with Parliament and the Protectorate to continue as a printer of Bibles after the Restoration. Although the excesses of Puritanism were swept away with the return of Charles II (1630-1685) to England in 1660, even that 'merry monarch' was politically astute enough to tell the clergy of London at his first meeting that he would 'make the Bible the rule of his life and government'. The reality of his governance, however, was different, summed up in his 1673 appointment of the layman Isaac Vossius (1618-1689) as residentiary canon of Windsor, who, the King said, 'would believe anything if only it was not in the Bible'. With the Civil War, Commonwealth, and Protectorate experiment still fresh in the collective national memory, there was a certain distaste for pulpit-pounding 'Bible Christians', whether clergy or laity. The result was that the Bible, while viewed as *an* authority for civilized living increasingly lost its pre-eminence in England as the only source. As for the Bible itself, no new revisions were undertaken from 1660 to 1710, though there were some 237 editions printed during that time, all essentially identical. The text, reflecting the society it served, was meant to be stable.

36   *The Holy Bible, Containing the Old Testament and the New: Newly Translated out of the Original Tongues.* London: Assigns of J. Bill, Thomas Newcomb and Henry Hills, 1684.

This copy of the Scriptures is in fact a piracy with a false imprint. As has been noted, the right to print the Bible belonged to the King's printer (or Parliament's as was the case during the Protectorate) as well as the presses of Oxford and Cambridge. Technically, only those Bibles printed in England by those three entities could be circulated within the country's borders. One of the unintended consequences of such a lucrative monopoly was the appearance of illegal copies, like this one, printed elsewhere (often in the Netherlands) but with what appears to be a legitimate imprint, thereby allowing it to be sold without raising suspicion, and without profits going into the pockets of the authorized printers. The Amsterdam printer and rabbi Joseph Athias (1635-1700), for example, claimed to have printed over a million contraband English Bibles, for which the States of Holland actually gave him an exclusive fifteen-year privilege in 1670. At the end of the century, speculators began to redirect their investment away from the continental pirates to the newly reinvigorated Oxford University Press, which had begun to print the Bible in earnest, thereby representing the first real domestic competition for the business with the King's Printer.

37   *The Holy Bible, Containing the Old Testament and the New, Newly Translated out of the Original Tongues and with the Former Translations Diligently Compared and Revised by His Majestie's Special Command.* [Amsterdam], 1708.

The subtitle to this 'hybrid' King James Bible describes it as being 'with most profitable annotations upon all the hard places, and other things of great importance; which notes have never before been set forth with this new translation; but are now placed in due order with great care and industrie'. Known simply as 'Canne's Bible', this edition was first produced at Amsterdam in 1642 with the marginal notes of Junius and the Geneva Bible added by the radical dissenter and exile, John Canne (d. 1667), who was leader of the Brownist sect in that city. With the Civil War, Canne returned to England and in June 1653, successfully petitioned Parliament for permission to reprint the Bible with his notes, after it had become clear that efforts to completely retranslate the Bible by the Puritans had failed. With the Restoration, he fled back to Amsterdam where some two thousand of his Bibles were sold in 1663 alone. Owing to the number of errors in his books, Canne was not highly regarded as a printer; nevertheless his Bible continued to be reprinted into the nineteenth century.

38   *The Cambridge Paragraph Bible.* Cambridge: University Press, 1873.

Throughout the eighteenth and nineteenth centuries there had been efforts to standardize the King James Bible by correcting earlier printing errors and allowing for better translations of certain phrases within the text. The most important of these was the edition achieved by Benjamin Blayney in 1769. It was not without its own errors, however, but it did achieve a level of standardization that lasted until the publication of the *Cambridge Paragraph Bible* in 1873. One of the most significant developments in this latter undertaking by Oxford and Cambridge scholars was that, for the first time, the King James text would be arranged contextually in paragraphs, allowing the text to be read more narratively. Under the direction of Frederick H.A. Scrivener (1813-1891), the language was strictly compared with the 1611 edition, archaic spelling was modernized, inaccurate phrases corrected, and the marginal notes improved. This revision likely served as a model for the committee which, at that very moment, was working on a new English translation of the Bible that would appear in 1881, intended as a replacement for the old King James. Scrivener was himself a member of the New Testament committee. The volume on display was presented to the University of Toronto by the University of Cambridge 'to aid in replacing the loss caused by the Disastrous Fire of February the 14th, 1890'.

39 *The Holy Bible.* London: Oxford University Press; Printed at Toronto by the Ryerson Press, 1943-1944.

In 1943, C.H. Dickinson, book steward for the United Church of Canada Publishing House, observed that logistical problems caused by World War II were forcing Canadian presses to focus on the home front and lessen their dependence on foreign suppliers, like the British. One lucrative enterprise that emerged as a result of the crisis was this first printing of a Canadian King James Bible. Since the time of the Stuarts, the right to print the Authorized Version of Bible for use within the British Empire belonged only to those appointed by the monarch, and to them alone. The reason generally given for this was that it was believed to be a function of the Coronation Oath that the Crown should ensure that the Bible was printed without error; for that reason letters patent were issued only to those who enjoyed the monarch's trust. This privilege, however, pertained only to the King James Bible. As William Murray, Lord Mansfield (1705-1793) ruled in *Millar v. Taylor* (1769), 'the copy of the Hebrew Bible, the Greek Testament, or the Septuagint does not belong to the King: it is common. But the English translation he bought: therefore it has been concluded to be his property. If any man should turn the Psalms,

or the writings of Solomon, or Job, into verse, the King could not stop the printing or sale of such a work: it is the author's work. The king has no power or control over the subject-matter.' Until 1944, Canadians, like other subjects of the Empire, had always depended on the supply of Bibles printed and bound in England and then shipped for sale and distribution around the globe. Since World War II had made access to paper and ink difficult, the project was contracted to the United Church of Canada Publishing House, Ryerson Press, which printed an initial run of thirty thousand copies from British plates which had been made in 1943 and exported to Canada the following year. On 20 April 1944, Dickinson proudly reported to the United Church Board of Publication that 'a printing and pub-lishing enterprise of national interest during the past year has been the first printing of the Bible in Canada. Our House has had the honour of doing this work for the Oxford University Press'. The publication of the Authorized Version of the Bible has remained in Canada ever since.

On loan from a private collection.

Fine Printing & Binding
of the English Bible

'Does the Bible belong to ecclesiastical authorities or to all of God's people?' Fundamentally, that was *the* question of the early sixteenth century. What is the place of Scripture in our world and in our lives? The reformers believed that the Bible should be accessible to everyone; the establishment believed that popes, councils, and universities were necessary to interpret the Bible for the masses. Strict control was sought. The debate in 1519 between Martin Luther and the Catholic theologian Johann Eck highlighted this division. Eck asked Luther how people could possibly understand the Bible on their own; Luther gave the controversial reply that 'a simple layman with Scripture' is more powerful than either pope or council.

Regardless of whichever side of the ecclesiastical divide one found oneself standing, the very beauty of the Scriptures themselves remained a point of agreement. Jerome's fine verse became a model of excellence for Latin prose. The reformer William Tyndale devoted his life to making the Bible accessible to the English nation in a manner so clear and artistic that his work became the foundation of the King James Bible itself. It was his prayer that 'the ploughman might read the Gospels at his plough and the weaver at his shuttle, and maybe even commercial travellers might learn to tell the tales to one another'. The redactors of the King James Bible polished each phrase of the ancient text until it began to sing, and then gathered them all together with a balance and reverence that has given enduring impact. How can one not be moved upon reading 'Arise, shine; for thy light has come and the glory of the Lord is risen upon thee' or 'They shall beat their swords into ploughshares, and their spears into pruning hooks: nation shall not lift up sword against nation; neither shall they learn war any more'?

This hugely significant shift in approach to the Bible was, of course, taking place against the backdrop of the Renaissance which had a profound effect on the way that people perceived the world and their relationship with God. It was also a period when the Church sought out great artists to create works that are now world treasures. Their art did not require interpretations by scholars or theologians or clergy to be appreciated. As the centuries advanced, their ranks swelled to include the finest printers and binders who turned their attention to the Sacred Word itself.

These books, with their elegant types, fine paper, and exquisite bindings are also treasures. They intimately 'hold' the words of Scripture both literally and figuratively. They provide at once, historical beauty, reverence, worship, and a tribute to the Glory of God; but they offer more. As works of art they go beyond words. They communicate meaning in an imaginative and unique way that is accessible to everyone. In this way they 'capture' the meaning, spirit, and richness of the Bible, as if to answer for evermore, the question concerning the place of Scripture in the world. These works created by ordinary but talented men and women truly do embrace the Word.

The Very Reverend Douglas Stoute,
Rector of the Cathedral of St James, Dean of Toronto

40 *The Holy Bible, Containing the Old Testament and the New.* London: John Bill and Christopher Barker, Printers to the King, 1666. (KJV)

This King James Bible is bound in contemporary black goatskin, and decorated with a gilt three-line fillet and dentelle border, with a sumptuously blind-tooled central panel. It is 'cottage style' meaning that the top and bottom of the central panel slope away from a broken centre, forming a sort of gable. In its day it would have been described as 'edges extraordinary' meaning a gilt border with multiple panels that displayed elaborate interlacing decoration, and according to one surviving price list from 1669, would have cost five shillings to make. As is often the case with these bindings, spaces are busy with arabesques, sprays, and branches in

combination with lacework, generally executed by the same small tools used to make the other ornaments. Originating in France around 1630, this style became popular with English bookbinders even before the Restoration and remained fashionable until about 1710. As late as 1822, it was still used to decorate devotional books and almanacs. It should also be noted that the printer of this volume, Christopher Barker, was the grandson of the first Christopher Barker who had obtained the patent to print the Bible during the reign of Queen Elizabeth I in 1577, and was son of Robert Barker, printer of the first edition of the King James Bible. The family's patent was finally lost in 1709 to Thomas Newcomb and Henry Hills, and transferred shortly thereafter to John Baskett.

41 *The Holy Bible, Containing the Old and New Testaments.* Edinburgh: Printed by Richard Watkins, one of His Majesty's Printers, 1744-1746. (KJV)

42 *The Holy Bible, containing the Old and New Testaments.* Edinburgh: Printed by Alexander Kincaid, His Majesty's Printer, [1766]. (KJV)

The King James Bible was not printed in Scotland until 1628. The primary concern of the General Assembly of the Church of Scotland thereafter was to control the large number of printing errors that were creeping into the text, whether through imports or domestically produced copies. After 1717, it became the duty of a specially appointed commission to ensure the accuracy of the Scriptures within the country. While the Elders were busy seeing to their corrections, Scottish

craftsmen had turned their attention to the beauty of the Bible's covers. Drawing upon European 'fan bindings' as their inspiration, Scottish bookbinders developed the 'wheel binding', examples of which are displayed here. Introduced to the country about 1725, they remained popular until the 1770s, and are most often found on Bibles and presentation copies of academic dissertations. Typical of this style, both books also possess Dutch gilt endpapers. It is perhaps surprising that so opulent a binding would have emerged in Presbyterian Scotland of all places in the British Isles; but, with the absolute ban on images of any kind from their strict Calvinist society, it is perhaps appropriate that the focus of what art was permitted should have been trained on enshrining the Word itself.

43 *The Holy Bible, Containing the Old and New Testaments.* Oxford: Printed by T. Baskett, 1756. (KJV)

44 *The Holy Bible, Containing the Old Testament and the New.* Oxford: T. Wright and W. Gill, and sold by S. Crowder, London, and W. Jackson, Oxford, 1774. (KJV)

These two Bibles display another binding style popularized by Scottish artisans in the eighteenth century, namely the 'herring-bone'. The name quite clearly derives from the decoration of the central panel which had the appearance of the spine of

84

a fish. Unlike the wheel binding, there is no obvious precedent for this style either on the Continent or in England, but once again, it appears almost exclusively on Bibles and dissertations. Whether these two items from the Fisher collection were actually the product of Scottish binders is uncertain since they do not display two of the most typical ornaments used north of the border, namely the distinctive pear or palm leaf design. The presence of St Andrew's crosses on both spines may argue for a Scottish provenance, though this type of decoration is also found on Irish and English bindings of the period. As opposed to the wheel-binding, however, for all of its inherent beauty, the herring-bone has been criticized for displaying rigidity and stiffness of execution.

45 *The Holy Bible, Containing the Old Testament and the New.* Cambridge: John Baskerville, 1763. (KJV)

This beautifully printed Bible is considered Baskerville's *magnum opus.* John Baskerville (1706-1775) was arguably the greatest English printer and typographer of the eighteenth century. He hailed from Birmingham and produced his first book in 1757 - an edition of Virgil. While his type fonts were praised abroad, they initially found little appreciation at home in England. As a result he almost ceased his printing enterprises in the year that this King James Bible appeared. In the end, however, Baskerville's technique did markedly influence the printing trade, especially his insistence that 'pure' typography was the only way to produce fine books. Ironically, Baskerville was a professed agnostic who stated in his 1773 will: 'I consider revelation . . . exclusive of the scraps of morality casually intermixt with it, to be the most impudent abuse of common sense'. Nevertheless, his folio Bible, printed at the Cambridge Press where Baskerville was University Printer, was magnificent. The paper is smooth and even, the ink glossy, the workmanship of highest quality. Not surprisingly it has been described as 'one of the finest books of its, or any other century.' A letter from fellow printer and friend Benjamin Franklin was included in

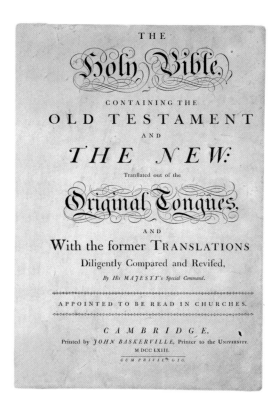

the advertisement for the Bible to promote its sale. Unhappily, the edition of 1250 copies was a financial failure; delayed in production, a third of the copies were unsold and eventually remaindered. Owing to Franklin's patronage, however, Baskerville's type became well-known and highly favoured in the American colonies.

46 *The Holy Bible, Containing the Old and New Testaments.* London: Printed by G.E. Eyre and W. Spottiswoode, 1847. (KJV)

This Victorian Bible has an ornate papier-mâché binding that imitates the appearance of ebony. In their love for all things medieval, the Victorians often took the rich floral and geometric designs carved on tombs for their inspiration, as well

as the architectural features found in cathedrals and parish churches throughout England. One attraction of such a binding was that it indulged the Victorian passion for making things appear to be other than what they are. In this case, the setting and style of Christ with his hand raised in blessing could easily have been a panel from a stone roodscreen. Religious motifs and images were commonly worked into the bindings, and it appears that it was specifically on Bibles that papier-mâché first made its appearance in England in the 1840s. This Bible is certainly among the earliest specimens. Such bindings were made from a combination of papier-mâché, plaster, and possibly antimony laid onto a metal framework. Owing to their complexity it has been suggested that a minimum run of one thousand would have been made in order to recoup the costs of production. Adding to its opulence, the edges of this particular Bible have also been gauffered. In this process, the gilded edges are decorated using heated finishing tools or rolls, indenting small, repeated patterns. Although gauffering had its origins in sixteenth century Germany, it declined in popularity from the middle of the seventeenth century, but was revived again in England in the middle of the nineteenth century when it was used most elaborately on devotional texts like this one. On display is a copy from Upper Canada College, Toronto presented on 9 August 1848 for third prize in 'Scripture and Learning' to J. Bethune (probably Charles James Bethune, son of Alexander Bethune, second Anglican Bishop of Toronto).

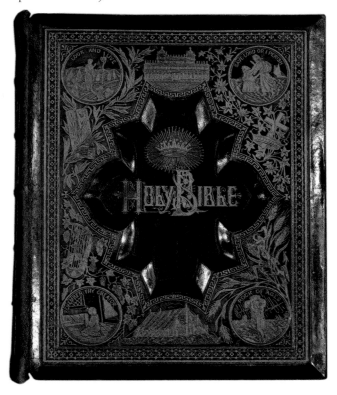

47 *The Holy Bible: Containing the Old and New Testaments.* Paris, Ont.: John S. Brown, ca. 1880. (KJV)

48 *The Holy Bible Containing the Entire Canonical Scriptures.* Woodstock, N.B.: Thompson & Co., ca. 1880. (Haydock Bible.)

Both of these large Family Bibles were probably printed in the United States and imported into Canada. Bound in original publisher's full leather panel bindings, ornate gilt decorations adorn the boards and spines of both, and illustrations are liberally scattered throughout with numerous full-page engravings, chromolithographs, and maps. Besides the texts themselves, the differences between the two are principally iconographic and are easily discernible. The covers of the King James Bible distributed out of Paris, Ontario reference the Scriptures directly, and include the tablets of the Law, David's harp, the serpent in the desert, and Christ and Peter upon the waters. Two devotional vignettes at the bottom depict a child at prayer with the motto 'Remember thy Creator', and a penitent clinging to a cross with the words 'Rock of Ages' above its vertical shaft. In contrast the Roman Catholic (Haydock) Bible from New Brunswick also contains Biblical scenes on its cover (including the descent from the Cross, da Vinci's Last Supper, and the procession of the Magi), but adds more typically Catholic imagery such as the Virgin and Child, the Immaculate Heart of Mary pierced by a sword, the IHS cipher of the Jesuits, a papal tiara, bishop's mitre, and croziers. Worked into the shaft of the Cross in gilt are also a chalice, shamrocks, and the Virgin's lily. The very covers of these Bibles, therefore, were both didactic and subtly propagandistic and, as Daniell notes, they became 'an essential piece of furniture in the American home'.

Given that the first King James Bible was not legally printed in Canada until 1944, it is necessary to explain an Ontario imprint on a Bible that appeared some sixty years earlier. In late nineteenth-century Canada, local booksellers generally received their stock from distributing agencies whose imprint usually appeared on the title-page. John S. Brown was the Methodist proprietor of a Paris 'Stationery and Fancy Goods Store' whose principal source for books was the National Publishing Company of Philadelphia. In the case of this King James Bible, a title-page bearing Brown's name has been tipped in at the front, likely replacing the original. The same is the case for the Woodstock Haydock Catholic Bible; it too was one of numerous books published by the National Publishing Company of Philadelphia which received a local bookseller's imprint. Showing no prejudice towards his customers, John Brown carried it in Paris as well. It was a matter of good business, however, for the Company to cater to the religious tastes of its clients by providing distinct denominational bindings.

49 *Psalmi penitentiales.* Hammersmith: Printed by William Morris, at the Kelmscott Press, 1894.

This fine copy of the penitential Psalms in Latin verse and English paraphrase was printed on handmade linen paper in a limited edition of three hundred copies in December of 1894, at the same time that the renowned Kelmscott Chaucer was in production. The English text was actually found in a copy of the Little Hours of the Blessed Virgin penned at Gloucester about the year 1440, and then transcribed and edited by Frederick Startridge Ellis (1830-1901). The Gloucester manuscript was itself probably a copy of an earlier Kentish text. Ellis was criticized by later scholars for not faithfully reproducing his exemplar which is now in the Morgan Library. Furthermore, Morris and he disagreed over the editing process, especially in the choice of which modern English words best reflected Middle English syntax. Critics have since acknowledged, however, that the Kelmscott edition was not intended first and foremost for scholars, but for bibliophiles. The book is a magnificent specimen of the artistry of both William Morris (1834-1896) and his Kelmscott Press. Morris preferred to print his text within a strongly-defined text block, which was not always possible with poetry. Here, he clearly rose to the challenge, executing the book in a fine Chaucer type, with a simple woodcut margin of plants and vines. Bound in a plain quarter holland (blue paper on boards), the entire production cost seventy-one pounds, thirteen shillings with individual volumes selling for seven shillings and sixpence. In a rare expression of opinion concerning her husband's work, Mrs Morris described this book as one of her favourites.

50 *The English Bible: Containing the Old Testament & the New.* Hammersmith: Printed by T.J. Cobden-Sanderson & Emery Walker at the Doves Press, 1903-1905.

Issued in five volumes, the text used in this superb Bible was edited by the Reverend F.H. Scrivener in the 1870s. It is considered the finest example of the books produced at the legendary Doves Press that operated in Hammersmith between 1900 and 1917. T.J. Cobden-Sanderson (1840-1922) and Sir Emery Walker (1851-1933) had been associates of William Morris, and were among the primary exponents of the Arts and Crafts movement in printing. Cobden-Sanderson commissioned Walker to design the type seen here, based on that used by Nicolas Jenson (1420-1480) in his 1476 printing of Pliny's *Historia naturalis.* The perfection of paper, richness of ink, evenness of print, and quality of type all characterize the ideals of craftsmanship adopted by several significant fine printing establishments that flourished in Britain and North America at the turn of the twentieth century. The aim of their movement, whose advocates included Elbert Hubbard (1856-1915) in the United States and Elizabeth Yeats (1868-1940) in Ireland, was to recapture the beauty of books, especially as they were created in the late medieval and incunable eras. The Doves Bibles were issued by subscription, one volume at a time, with subscribers committed to purchasing the complete set. They are bound in their original full limp vellum with a gilt title on the spine. After the appearance of volume five in June 1905, the Press announced that the enormously successful edition was out of print. Owing to tensions within the partnership, the matrices used to form the magnificent types displayed in this Bible were thrown from Hammersmith Bridge into the Thames by Cobden-Sanderson in 1913; the types themselves followed in 1917. Not surprisingly, Doves Bibles remain among the most desirable publications to emanate from the Private Press movement.

IN THE BEGINNING

GOD CREATED THE HEAVEN AND THE EARTH. ❡ AND THE EARTH WAS WITHOUT FORM, AND VOID; AND DARKNESS WAS UPON THE FACE OF THE DEEP, & THE SPIRIT OF GOD MOVED UPON THE FACE OF THE WATERS. ❡ And God said, Let there be light: & there was light. And God saw the light, that it was good: & God divided the light from the darkness. And God called the light Day, and the darkness he called Night. And the evening and the morning were the first day. ❡ And God said, Let there be a firmament in the midst of the waters, & let it divide the waters from the waters. And God made the firmament, and divided the waters which were under the firmament from the waters which were above the firmament: & it was so. And God called the firmament Heaven. And the evening & the morning were the second day. ❡ And God said, Let the waters under the heaven be gathered together unto one place, and let the dry land appear: and it was so. And God called the dry land Earth; and the gathering together of the waters called he Seas: and God saw that it was good. And God said, Let the earth bring forth grass, the herb yielding seed, and the fruit tree yielding fruit after his kind, whose seed is in itself, upon the earth: & it was so. And the earth brought forth grass, & herb yielding seed after his kind, & the tree yielding fruit, whose seed was in itself, after his kind: and God saw that it was good. And the evening & the morning were the third day. ❡ And God said, Let there be lights in the firmament of the heaven to divide the day from the night; and let them be for signs, and for seasons, and for days, & years: and let them be for lights in the firmament of the heaven to give light upon the earth: & it was so. And God made two great lights; the greater light to rule the day, and the lesser light to rule the night: he made the stars also. And God set them in the firmament of the heaven to give light upon the earth, and to rule over the day and over the night, & to divide the light from the darkness: and God saw that it was good. And the evening and the morning were the fourth day. ❡ And God said, Let the waters bring forth abundantly the moving creature that hath life, and fowl that may fly above the earth in the open firmament of heaven. And God created great whales, & every living creature that moveth, which the waters brought forth abundantly, after their kind, & every winged fowl after his kind: & God saw that it was good. And God blessed them, saying, Be fruitful, & multiply, and fill the waters in the seas, and let fowl multiply in the earth. And the evening & the morning were the fifth day. ❡ And God said, Let the earth bring forth the living creature after his kind, cattle, and creeping thing, and beast of the earth after his kind: and it was so. And God made the beast of the earth after his kind, and cattle after their kind, and every thing that creepeth upon the

27

51 *Genesis: Twelve Woodcuts.* Soho: Nonesuch Press, 1924.

Paul Nash (1889-1946) was both a landscape artist as well as a producer of surrealist woodcuts, such as the ones that adorn this copy of the first chapter of the book of Genesis. He is perhaps best-known in Canadian artistic circles as one of the painters who worked alongside the Canadian forces at Vimy Ridge, and was subsequently chosen to work on the massive canvas of 'A Night Bombardment' in the National Gallery of Canada. In this book, one cannot help but sense that his experience of war has influenced his artistic style. Bold illustrations reflect the violent, cosmic mythology of the creation story, bearing such titles as 'The Void', 'The Face of the Waters', 'The Stars Also', and 'Contemplation'. Each imparts a strong sense of the epic within small but dramatic spaces. The book was printed in a limited edition of 375 copies on French-folded, uncut, hand-made, cream-coloured paper, with the sacred text printed in Rudolph Koch's Neuland type, here making its English debut. Nonesuch was a private press founded in

93

1923 by Francis Meynell (1891-1975) and David Garnett (1892-1981). Although they used a small Albion hand press to design the books, production was actually executed by commercial printers - in this case, the Curwen Press of London. The theory behind this somewhat unusual practice was that it would be easier and cheaper to obtain a fine-press product in this way without sacrificing the quality of workmanship.

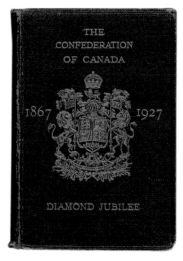

52 *The New Testament of Our Lord and Saviour Jesus Christ.* London, British and Foreign Bible Society, Printed at the University Press, Oxford, 1926. (KJV)

As previously noted, the Scottish wheel and herring-bone bindings were most often found on presentation copies of the Scriptures in the eighteenth century. The tradition of giving presentation copies of the Bible continued well into the twentieth century as gifts to mark the baptism of infants, graduation, marriage, and ordination. This copy of the New Testament was given to W. Chester S. McLure (1875-1955) upon his taking the Oath of Allegiance as a Member of the Legislative Assembly of Prince Edward Island in 1928, and is signed by F.L. Hazard, Justice of the Supreme Court of P.E.I. It is bound in dark maroon cloth with the arms of Canada and 'The Confederation of Canada, 1867-1927, Diamond Jubilee' stamped in gilt on the front cover.

53 *The Four Gospels of the Lord Jesus Christ.* Waltham Saint Lawrence, Berkshire: Printed and Published at the Golden Cockerel Press, 1931. (KJV)

This beautiful copy of the four Gospels was the collaborative result of some of the greatest book artists of the early twentieth century. Limited to five hundred copies which originally sold for eight guineas each, it was illustrated with decorations by Eric Gill (1882-1940), printed by Robert Gibbings (1889-1958) and his wife Moira, and hand bound by Sangorski and Sutcliffe. The compositors were Frank Young and Albert C. Cooper (1890-1989), the latter of whom was described by Gill as 'the (almost) infallible', so highly did he esteem his pressmanship. Chapter and verse enumeration are eliminated from the text, restoring a sense of narrative flow to the Authorized Version of the Gospels. It was the first book printed in the eighteen-point size of the new Golden Cockerel typeface which had been designed by Gill. For all of these reasons it arguably represents the summit of the early fine press movement. The process by which the design of the Bible unfolded is best described in the words of Gibbings himself:

> *I would spend hours with the compositors while they worked on the chapter headings or other occasions of decoration. Generally we would begin on the right of the page with a few words in the 36-point set in short lines of perhaps a half or a third of the measure. From the 36-point we would drop to the 24-point for another few short lines, then having achieved a blank shape on the left of the page that seemed to offer possibilities to the artist for his initial letters we would continue for a few full lines in 18-point capitals. From then on it would be straight-forward capitals and lower case until we reached the next site for a decoration. We had no rules for the putting together of these varied sizes of capitals. We allowed the type almost complete control, improvising the tune according to the note suggested. It came about, therefore, that almost every blank space left for the artist was different and that is one reason, I believe, for the liveliness which runs through the book.*

The Golden Cockerel Gospels is most frequently compared to the Doves Bible, and was described as 'a flower among the best products of English romantic genius[;] it is also surely, thanks to its illustrator, Eric Gill, the book among all books in which roman type has been best mated with any kind of illustration'. Particularly striking are Gill's woodcuts which display a great deal of movement against open, white spaces. He completed the fifty-eight principal engravings between 13 December 1930 and 21 October 1931. One of the more interesting depicts the triumphal entry into Jerusalem introducing the passage that begins, 'And when they drew nigh unto Jerusalem'. Gill, who had been received into the Roman Catholic Church in 1913, had inexplicably used the text of the Douai-Rheims Bible which begins, 'Now when they drew nigh to Jerusalem' when preparing his original design. Here he skillfully reworked the image of Christ, whose hand now rests on the crossbar of the 'A' rather than on an 'N'.

THE

HOLY BIBLE

Containing the Old and New
Testaments : Translated out
of the Original Tongues and
with the former Translations
diligently compared and revised by His Majesty's special
Command

Appointed to be read in Churches

OXFORD
Printed at the University Press
1935

54 *The Holy Bible: Containing the Old and New Testaments: Translated out of the Original Tongues and with the Former Translations Diligently Compared and Revised by His Majesty's special Command.* Oxford: University Press, 1935. (KJV)

This superb lectern Bible was designed and executed by one of the greatest book artisans of the twentieth century, Bruce Rogers (1870-1957), and has a strong Canadian connection. Its origins are to be found in the desire of King George V (1865-1936) to present a suitable copy of the Bible to the memorial chapel being built by the Canadian government to honour the fallen soldiers of Ypres. The royal librarian, O.F. Morshead (1893-1977), knew of nothing worthy of the occasion, and so the task fell to Humphrey Milford (1877-1952) of the Oxford University Press to create a truly noble book. Rogers was engaged, and he modified and compressed his new Centaur type so that the final result would fall within the 1250-page limit stipulated by the Press. The title-page alone saw numerous revisions with the words 'Holy Bible' redrawn up to eight times and photo-engraved on copper, cut on wood, and then on brass. The final result places this Bible at the head of all of Rogers's achievements. Minimally decorated, the glory of this book is its clear, rich type. It is the epitome of Rogers's own philosophy of printing as he expressed it some eight years earlier. 'A beautiful book should first be an efficient instrument', he wrote; 'it should be legible and easy to read. It may at the same time be a work of art, with a beauty and personality of its own'.

55 *The Holy Bible, Containing the Old and New Testaments.* Oxford: University Press, 1953. (KJV)

Popularly known as the 'Coronation Bible', this book was printed under the direction of Charles Batey, Printer to the University of Oxford. Among its many distinguishing characteristics is the fact that the book was the work of a single compositor. While the vast majority of these Bibles were printed on regular paper, an additional twenty-five were printed on Oxford India paper, of which Fisher's copy is number seventeen. (The Queen took her Oath on copy number one.) The choice of India paper for the limited edition was not merely aesthetic, but was linked to the logistics of the ceremony itself. Standard issue paper, it was believed, would have made the book too bulky to be used gracefully, while the light India paper would be more easily manoeuvred. Fisher's copy belonged to Vincent Massey (1887-1967), eighteenth Governor-General of Canada, who represented the nation at the Coronation. The book is most memorable, for its striking binding. It was designed by the accomplished engraver and artist, Lynton Lamb (1907-1977), who had studied bookbinding under Douglas Cockerell (1870-1945) and was charged with the task of redesigning the bindings for Oxford's Bibles and prayer books. In preparing the design of the Bible, Lamb was concerned that dec-

oration should follow structure. He wrote that 'if one has taken a great deal of care over sewing the sheets to the cords, rounding the back, and making the boards true, one does not want to break down these effects by a contrary scheme of decoration. In this instance, the design of interlacing lines springs from the six cords on which the sheets are sewn; and while the gold lines are turned this way and that to catch the light, their pattern and that of the crowns and ciphers in blind and gold tooling powdered over the ground emphasizes the flatness and rectangularity of the boards.' The choice of a red-coloured binding was also made so that the book would blend in with the splendour of the other regalia. It boasts a scarlet goatskin cover on which Lamb imposed a large cream-coloured lozenge with the royal cipher, E II R, surmounted by a crown, in the centre. The intention was to attract the eye with a striking contrast, given that the book would be the focus of attention at one of the most pivotal moments in the liturgy. The actual binding was executed by Sangorski and Sutcliffe.

Paraphrases, Primers, & Peculiarities

I grew up in a minister's family where family devotions and a daily reading of the Bible were the norm. One of my earliest memories comes from a picture in a children's version of the Bible. The picture, as I remember it, portrayed a scowling Martha glowering over a half kitchen door at Mary sitting in the living room listening to Jesus. As an adult I now know the inaccuracies of that picture, but to my astonishment I also realize how much it has had an enduring effect, so much so that when my husband suggested the name Martha for our daughter it was vehemently rejected with no possibility of reconsideration. The saying, 'a picture is worth a thousand words' was particularly true in my case.

Throughout the centuries people have used the Bible, often in surprising and delightful ways, to show their devotion to the Word of God. Whether through map books, pop-up Bibles, Thumb Bibles, miniature Bibles or colourful pictures the desire is to educate, to help the reader appreciate, memorize, remember and live the story.

Distinctive and creative formats have been used to present the Bible to children and youth. In their creation there is the earnest desire to engage children early so that the Biblical narrative becomes very simply a part of life. However it is serious business for in telling the story, other things can happen. Pictures form an indelible imprint on any mind but particularly a young one and can just as easily skew the story as exemplify its truth.

I now have a granddaughter and my desire is to pass on to her my love of the Biblical stories, to help her understand their importance for a life that is lived fully and meaningfully. At present I have been scouring book stores looking for a creative re-telling that expresses what it will mean for her to live knowing God's love personally and instill in her a desire to love her neighbour wherever that neighbour is to be found. To my delight there are still pop-up books, miniature books, and since she is only eleven months old, even stain-proof books that tell that story!

The Reverend Dr. J. Dorcas Gordon,
Principal and Associate Professor Biblical Interpretation
and Preaching, Knox College, and Grandmother of Ava.

56 *The Booke of Psalmes, Collected into English Meeter.* London: Printed for the Company of Stationers, 1610.

The paraphrases of the Book of Psalms by Thomas Sternhold (1500-1549) and John Hopkins (1521-1570) assumed a central role in Protestant worship beginning in the middle of the sixteenth century. As the subtitle to this particular volume states, the text was versified from the Hebrew original, and was explicitly intended to be sung before or after Morning and Evening Prayer, as well as before and after the sermon. The paraphrases were also meant to be sung by families 'for their godly solace and comfort, laying apart all ungodly songs and ballads, which tend only to the nourishment of vice, and corrupting of youth.' As early as 1539 Miles Coverdale had adapted German Lutheran hymns and tunes in his *Goostly Psalms,* but his book was immediately suppressed by Henry VIII who was opposed to the works of the continental reformers. The tradition of singing the psalms in metre, however, had been quickly established. Thomas Sternhold had served as Groom of the Robes to both Henry VIII and his son Edward and would have been intimately familiar with Coverdale's efforts. A committed Protestant, his *Certayne Psalmes Chosen out of the Psalter of Dauid* was first printed in 1549 and would have an enormous influence over the development of English worship and hymn-singing in both Britain and North America. Originally it included only nineteen of the sacred poems in metre. In 1556 the Marian exiles combined his paraphrases with those of Hopkins, an Anglican minister, and the resulting book was the first English text printed in Geneva. It was not until 1562, however, that the printer John Day published a

second edition that featured all 150 psalms. Over the centuries, other composers set the Psalms to new tunes, but it was Sternhold and Hopkins who dominated the genre into the nineteenth century, especially in rural Britain, in spite of the fact that their poetry has been described as doggerel. By 1852 there had been over a thousand separate editions, with the Sternhold and Hopkins Psalms reproduced at the back of every version of the Geneva Bible after 1560, as well as in most editions of the Book of Common Prayer. Their metrical Psalms have faded in popularity over the past century, though the 'Old Hundredth' is still sung lustily in Protestant and Catholic congregations the world over.

57 John Lloyd (1638-1687). *A Good Help for Weak Memories, or, The Contents of every Chapter in the Bible in Alphabetical Dysticks.* London: Thomas Helder, 1671.

In this book, John Lloyd and his unnamed collaborators have taken the contents of the Bible, and summarized every chapter in rhyming couplets called 'dysticks'. As

explained in the preface, the book is intended to help boys and girls, aged ten years and upwards, to memorize the Scriptures. Thus each couplet begins with a letter of the alphabet which coincides with its chapter's position in a given book of the Bible. The rhyme for the first chapter of Genesis, therefore, begins with 'a', 'All's made in six days'; the second chapter with 'b', 'Blest is the Sabbath', and so forth. Thus 'when he hath learned twenty dysticks or more, examine him of particular passages in the chapters he hath past.' In theory, upon completion of these exercises, children would essentially possess a mental concordance to the Bible, so that they could quote chapter and verse at will for the edification of their elders and fellows. The idea for the book is based on the principle that rhyme is a natural *aide-de-mémoire.* Lloyd himself cautions, however, that 'if thou expectest a poetical flash, thou wilt be disappointed'; the rhymes, in fact, were not especially good. As one modern commentator observes, 'doubtless this was a noble undertaking, but hardly likely to lead its poor victims, whatever it might do for their "weak memories", to a love either for verse or the Bible'. The book was never reprinted.

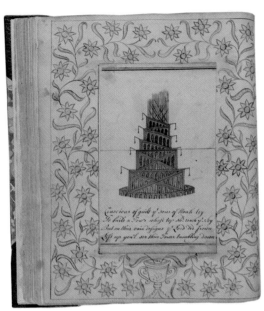

58　Robert Dodsley. [On Biblical Subjects: Poems, Histories, Meditations, Prayers] England, early 18th century.

Precise information about this flap-book manuscript is sadly elusive, save that the coloured illustrations are variously signed either R. Dodsley or Robt. Dodsley. Clearly intended for the instruction of children in Bible stories, the book combines a paraphrase of some of the most interesting Scriptural accounts with numerous scenes from both the Old and New Testaments. In most cases, flaps cover the pictures so that the reader's first view is of the beginning of a particular narrative such as the construction of the Tower of Babel or Noah leading the animals into his Ark. Upon lifting the flap one sees the end of the story - the destruction of the Tower, Moses offering a thanksgiving sacrifice after the Flood. While it may be tempting to attribute the work to Robert Dodsley (1703-1764) the famous publisher, poet, playwright, and editor, it more likely belongs to his father Robert (1681-1750) who was a school master at the Free School of Mansfield in Nottinghamshire. If that is the case, then this manuscript is all the more interesting since it predates the Sunday School movement of Robert Raikes (1736-1811) and Thomas Stock (1750-1803) which began towards the end of the eighteenth century. It certainly is consistent with the pedagogy evident in Lloyd's *A Good Help for Weak Memories* and reflects the emerging new educational theories that were influencing English teachers in the light of the revolutionary treatise of John Locke (1632-1704), *Some Thoughts concerning Education* (1693). In this book Locke acknowledges that the Bible has long been used as the principal text for the instruction of youths in their studies, but cautions that 'the promiscuous reading of it through by chapters as they lie in order, is so far from being of any advantage to children, either for the perfecting their reading, or principling their religion, that perhaps a worse could not be found'. He goes on to advise, however, that

> *. . . there are some parts of the Scripture which may be proper to be put into the hands of a child to engage him to read; such as are the story of Joseph and his brethren, of David and Goliath, of David and Jonathan, &c. and others that he should be made to read for his instruction, as that, What you would have others do unto you, do you the same unto them; and such other easy and plain moral rules, which being fitly chosen, might often be made use of, both for reading and instruction together.*

Dodsley's manuscript follows this basic principle, providing his young readers with enjoyable and exciting Bible stories, poems, and short histories, all of which prepare the mind to encounter the Scriptures which would be heard read at home and in church, and then pored over in adulthood.

59 *The Bible in Miniuture [sic], or, A Concise History of the Old & New Testaments.* London: Printed for Elizabeth Newbery, 1780.

60 *The Bible in Miniature, or, A Concise History of the Old & New Testaments.* London, 1812.

Miniature Bibles and Thumb Bibles form separate genera within the category of 'miniature books'. The term 'Thumb Bible' was first coined in 1849 as a 'picturesque, if vague, generic description of any very diminutive book' whose text is essentially Biblical. Specifically, miniature Bibles contain all of, or selections from, one of the standard versions of the Scriptures, while Thumb Bibles, like the two displayed here, are paraphrases intended principally, though not exclusively, for the use of children. The earliest English example of this genre dates from 1601 when John Weever's *An Agnus Dei*, a rhyming summary of the Scriptures, was published. The intent behind publications such as these was to expose the young to Bible stories as a preparation for tackling the more complicated Biblical texts as they grew older. Among the most familiar and popular English Thumb Bibles was Elizabeth Newbery's 1780 edition with its typical trade binding of crimson or green goatskin, elaborate gilt tooling, and the sacred monogram in the centre. The

Newbery family had been in the business of promoting children's literature since 1744 when John Newbery published *A Little Pretty Pocket Book*. Not surprisingly, illustrations figure prominently in Thumb Bibles, ranging from crude woodcuts to elegant engravings. So popular were these little books that some three hundred different editions were printed in the almost three hundred years spanning 1601 to 1890.

61 *The New Testament of Our Lord and Saviour Jesus Christ*. Oxford: Printed at the University Press, by S. Collingwood and Co., 1839.

This miniature Bible is bound together with *Proper Lessons to be Read at Morning & Evening Prayer on the Sundays and other Holy-days throughout the Year.* The reason for this combination was to assist the worshipper at Divine Service in the Church of England. Thus, references made by a preacher to other texts in the New Testament could easily be consulted, even though the set lessons for the day may have been taken from other parts of the Bible. Their diminutive character allowed for greater portability to and from the Liturgy, though the size of print may have presented a challenge to even the most youthful eyes at Evensong. This copy, for example, is printed in diamond type which translates as 4.5-point.

62 *A Curious Hieroglyphick Bible*. London: Thomas Hodgson, 1788.

The purpose of this beautiful little book was actually twofold. On the one hand, like the Thumb Bible, it was intended to introduce children to the adult world of the Scriptures. On the other, however, it was simply meant to teach them to read, playing the role of a modern rebus puzzle. Not surprisingly it was dedicated 'to the parents, guardians, and governesses of Great Britain and Ireland' and reflects the novel educational theories that were seeping into English society, introduced by philosophers like John Locke. In his preface, Hodgson offers the following

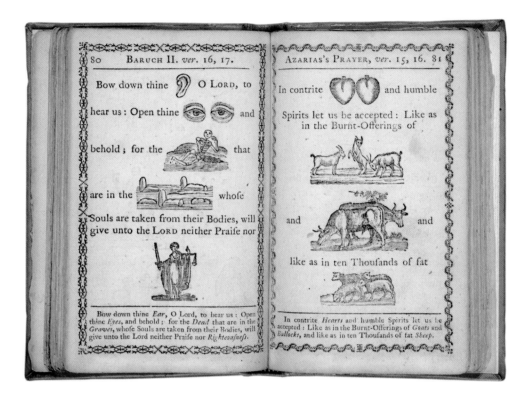

advice: 'Let the proper time never slip, when young infants show an inclination to receive instruction; but don't compel children to learn certain tasks in certain measured hours, for such compulsion, or constraint, is oftener an obstacle than an encouragement towards learning the necessary and useful sciences'. The books were simply designed and 'represented with emblematical figures, for the amusement of youth'; they also included short biographies of the Evangelists, and were illustrated throughout. The young reader was supposed to cover the key at the bottom of the page, and 'translate' the Scriptures using the printed images, thereby teaching themselves to read. Some five hundred woodcuts attributed to Thomas Bewick are used throughout to relate familiar stories from both the Old and New Testaments. So popular was this text that some twenty editions were published between 1783 and 1812.

63 *The Holy Bible Containing the Old and New Testaments, Embossed for the Use of the Blind.* Glasgow: Printed in the Asylum at the Institution Press, by John Alston, 1839-1840.

At the beginning of the nineteenth century scholars around the world were still trying to devise a system that would facilitate reading for the blind. In 1832, the Edinburgh Society of Arts awarded a gold medal to Dr Edmund Fry, of London, for the design and execution of a plain, raised roman letter which, with subsequent modifications, became popular in Britain and North America. John Alston (1778-1846), Treasurer of the Glasgow Asylum for the Blind, took Fry's type and altered it further. His principal motivation in doing so was to make religious texts accessible to his blind charges. To that end he established a printing press at the Asylum which produced these first English copies of the New Testament for the blind in 1840. With the support of the Scottish Bible Society and the Society for the Promotion of Christian Knowledge, he was able to defray the enormous expense of the project, and his edition of the Scriptures proved to be successful. It eventually included the Old Testament as well, with his complete Bible comprising nineteen volumes in total. So important was the work being done in Glasgow that a contemporary described that city as 'the fountain head of all works for the blind, save those published in America'. Alston's types were cut in very sharp, thin faces in two sizes, 'Great Primer' for ordinary use and 'Double Pica' for learners and older readers whose fingers for a variety of reasons had difficulty with the smaller forms. It was Alston's type that was used at the School for the Blind in Paris before the adoption of Braille. The Fisher copy was presented by Alston to the Reverend Robert Burns for the library of Knox College, Toronto on 25 March 1845.

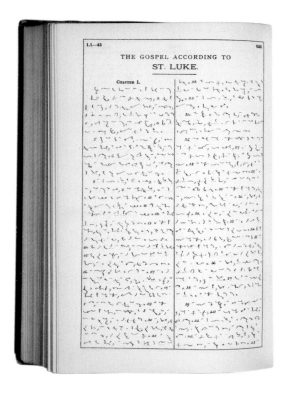

64 *The Holy Bible Containing the Old and New Testaments.* London: Isaac Pitman & Sons, 1890.

As the subtitle to this Bible notes, it is 'lithographed in the easy reporting style of phonography', that is, Pitman shorthand. At one time the Pitman system was the most popular form of shorthand in the English-speaking world. Invented by Sir Isaac Pitman (1813-1897), its ease of use made it extremely popular among stenographers. Pitman actually used the Bible as a way to teach his new method to the public, while simultaneously introducing much of the English-speaking world to the notion of distance education. In 1840 he began mailing postcards to students with instructions on how to use his shorthand. Their assignment was to apply his system to the Bible, transcribe set passages from the King James Version, and then return them to him for correction. In 1843, the Phonographic Correspondence Society was established, assuming responsibility of the correction of the students' work while at the same time laying the foundations for the Pitman Correspondence Colleges. Besides the Bible, a number of other works including *The Book of Common Prayer*, Bunyan's *Pilgrim's Progress*, and Bacon's *Essays* were eventually printed in it, generally from lithographs. In each case, Pitman's intention was that the student should read the shorthand text, write it out in English orthography, compare the results with the standard printed text, reverse the process, and repeat as long as there were errors. Hence, this 1890 publication is as much intended to be an exercise book as it is another vehicle for the Scriptures. The first published edition of the Pitman shorthand New Testament appeared in 1849 with a complete Bible the following year.

65   Chuck Fischer. *In the Beginning: the Art of Genesis. A Pop-up Book.* New York: Little, Brown and Company, 2008.

Pop-up books have been a staple of children's literature since the mid-nineteenth century, though their interactive appeal have ensured that few specimens have actually survived from that period. This latter-day example includes both ingenious three-dimensional spreads as well as accompanying narrative booklets. Inspired by a vintage copy of *The Golden Children's Bible*, artist and muralist Chuck Fischer designed the pop-ups by combining classic artworks with his own artistic creations, while the actual paper engineering was undertaken by Bruce Foster. On display is the Tower of Babel which extends to fifty-one centimetres in height, a rather remarkable a feat for a book which is itself only twenty-eight by twenty-three centimetres.

The English Bible
in North America

The Bible's extraordinary path in Indigenous North America has received little attention from Western academics, even religious academics. This seems to be related to its clearly non-Western trajectory among Indigenous Peoples; their approach has not often affirmed Western thought, religious or non-religious. One does not need to look at modern examples, like Vine Deloria's famous book, *God is Red*. The Scriptures have long played a key role in Indigenous resistance to colonialism, including such important examples as the Ghost Dance and the resistance of Louis Riel in the late 1800s.

Dramatic counter-narratives aside, the Bible had a more quiet, humble, and pervasive impact in most of Indigenous life. Many Indigenous people like to repeat an observation often attributed to Desmond Tutu: 'We got the Bible, and they got the land.' It reveals some of the complexity of these transactions, politically and spiritually. The Bible narratives have found a home among the People of the Land, following a path and pattern of its own, resonating with Native life, values, and vision. For many First Nations, if the Bible had not been translated into their language, there would be even fewer who speak it now. Though this is not necessarily the plan the colonial missionaries had in mind, it displays an important aspect of the way the Bible has become a Canadian book.

St. Innocent of Alaska and Moscow, in the mid-1800s, noted the close affinity that Indigenous Peoples had with the world of the New Testament, surpassing that of the so-called 'Christian' civilizations. Over time, the Scriptures have become a part of the Indigenous world, woven in with traditional teachings and stories, entering into a mutually illuminating relationship with Native stories, and paving the way, for many, to walk the ancient path of the elders in a way that allowed a full embrace of the future.

That Scripture has this great capacity - to inspire hope in desperate circumstance, to pave the way to a liveable future, even as it affirms the past - should encourage us today. But Indigenous spiritual experience and wisdom shows us something that should always be remembered and, we pray, cherished: the narrative of Scripture is still calling us today; it cannot be controlled or manipulated to serve the narrow plans of human beings, though we can expect that many will try just that. It will pursue a course that will illuminate and challenge us beyond all that we can expect or hope for. Though some may use it to oppress, it has the power to inspire communities of hope. The Bible is a book with an interesting past. It should have a much more interesting future.

The Right Reverend Mark Macdonald,
National Indigenous Bishop, Anglican Church of Canada.

66 *Ne yakawea yondereanayendaghkwa oghseragwegouh, neoni yakawea ne orighwadogeaghty yondatnekosseraghs, neoni tekarighwagehhadont.* London: Christopher Buckton, 1787.

The basic position of the Protestant colonial powers concerning evangelization in North America was that the truth of Christianity would be self-evident to those who could read the Bible in their own language. Thus, as early as 1649, Oliver Cromwell had established a society named 'the Corporation for the Promoting and Propagating of the Gospel of Jesus Christ in New England' and the first Algonquin New Testament was printed at Cambridge, Massachusetts in 1663. After the American Revolution, concern for the King's loyal native subjects did not wane, as this 1787 edition of the Book of Common Prayer demonstrates; besides the formal Liturgy of the Church of England it also included the first translation of any complete Biblical text printed in the Mohawk language. Thayendanegea,

FRONTISPIECE

better known as Joseph Brant (1742-1807) completed this translation of the Gospel of St Mark in 1774 while he was working under the direction of John Stuart of the Society for the Propagation of the Gospel at Fort Hunter in the old colony of New York. In 1781 Daniel Claus, an Indian interpreter and lieutenant in the Royal American Regiment, brought Brant's manuscript to England, and saw it incorporated into the Prayer Book at the expense of the British Government. The rationale for including the English and Mohawk translation together was ostensibly didactic as the preface to the Prayer Book states. 'Hereby the Indians will insensibly be made acquainted with the English language; and such White People in their vicinity as chuse to learn Mohawk will hence derive much assistance.' The volume also included nineteen engravings executed by James Peachey (d. 1797). Peachey had been a surveyor, draughtsman, army officer, and artist who had worked throughout the British colonies in North America both before and after the American Revolution. As this book demonstrates, he also tried his hand at book illustration in collaboration with the London printer Christopher Buckton. In 1786 he etched the frontispiece to Claus's *A Primer for the Use of the Mohawk Children,* and in the following year illustrated this volume. Peachey eventually returned to Canada where he executed portraits of Joseph Brant and his wife Catherine.

114

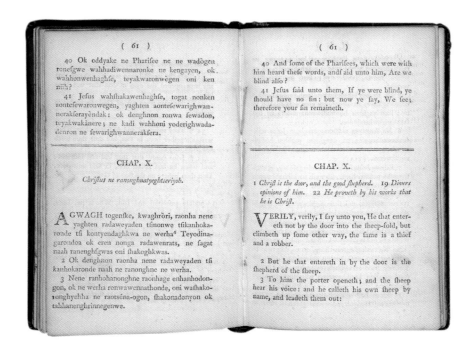

67 *Nene karighwiyoston tsinihorighhoten ne Saint John.* London: Printed for the British and Foreign Bible Society by Phillips & Fardon, 1804.

The rise of Evangelical movements in England at the end of the seventeenth century, led to the formation of several influential Bible societies across the country in the latter years of George III's reign. Among these were the English Baptist Society (1792), the London Missionary Society (1795), the Church Missionary Society (1799), the Religious Tract Society (1799), and the Methodist Missionary Society (1813). Although the primary impetus for the foundation of the British and Foreign Bible Society in the London Tavern on 7 March 1804 was to provide a copy of the Scriptures in Welsh, the initial result was actually this Mohawk and English diglot copy of the Gospel of St John. A note in the Society's 1807 records states that some two thousand copies, bound in calf, were produced at a cost of £204.9.6. The Gospel was translated by Teyoninhokarawen, who was known as John Norton (fl. 1784-1825), a Cherokee who had served as a Captain in the British army during the American Revolution. His translation was actually undertaken in Clapham while Norton was living with Lord Teignmouth, the first President of the Society. It is worthy of note that until 1800 the Bible had appeared, throughout all of its long history, in only sixty languages; by 1900 it had been translated into five hundred, and by 1925, 835, worldwide.

68 *Ne royadado kengh ty orighwadokenghty roghyadon S. Mark.* New York: New-York District Bible Society, M'Elrath & Bangs, Printers, 1829.

This copy of St Mark's Gospel in English and Mohawk was a reprint of Brant's 1787 edition first printed at London. The provision of a translation of the Scriptures in the native languages was an important part of the efforts to assimilate the native people of the New World into the transplanted culture of Europe. Since the indigenous population of North America did not have a written language, the very act of providing one, whether in syllabic or letter form, has been interpreted in more recent times, however, as a controversial act of enculturation over a traditional, oral society. To make this situation even more complicated, the fact that the text most often translated for them was the Judaeo-Christian Scriptures invested the Bible with a powerful totemic and symbolic value as well. As one missionary preacher put it, 'The Great Spirit has not given you any such Book, but he has given it to us'. Whether the intention was to press their advantage or simply spread the Gospel, Bible Societies began to spring up across the United States after the 'Second Great Awakening' of 1797, with the express purpose of providing the Word in English as well as the native languages. Overseeing the activity of the many local chapters was the American Bible Society (ABS), established in 1816. In 1829, the year that this diglot copy of St Mark appeared, the ABS printed 360,000 English Bibles alone.

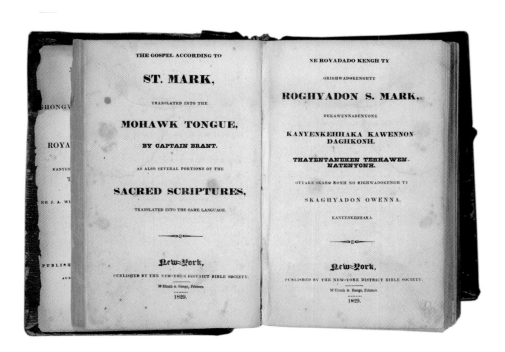

69 *The New Testament of Our Lord and Saviour Jesus Christ.* York (U.C.): Robert
Stanton, [1830?].

The printing of this intriguing copy of the King James New Testament raises more
questions than it actually settles. As William Lyon Mackenzie's 1827 broadside
Beware of Wooden Nutmegs!! makes perfectly clear, 'Bibles and Testaments in the English language are permanent copy right works in the hands of the King's printers
and the two universities [i.e. Oxford and Cambridge]'. Since there is no record of
permission granted by the Crown for Stanton to print this New Testament, and
the jealousy with which the appointed British printers guarded their royal prerog-
ative, it is mysterious how this copy came to have an Upper Canadian imprint some
113 years before the first acknowledged 'authorized' Canadian printing appeared.
Robert Stanton (1794-1866) was a Canadian merchant and magistrate appointed
King's Printer at York (later Toronto) by Sir Peregrine Maitland in 1826. Stereo-

type plates of the New Testament, most likely American in origin, were certainly in circulation in Upper Canada at this time, since the Kingston printer James Macfarlane advertised a 'duodecimo stereotype edition' in 1829. Four years later, a set of plates was offered for sale in St Thomas. Is it possible that Stanton could have imported American stereotype plates of the New Testament into the colony, in spite of Mackenzie's recent warnings that they 'cannot be admitted from the United States to Canada'? One possible explanation is that in his capacity as 'King's Printer' he may have legitimately thought that it was his right to print the Authorized Version of the Scriptures, in order to combat the illegal trade in American Testaments. Whatever the case may be, it is also clear that Stanton did not continue to print the King James Bible after this venture.

On loan from Victoria University - Emmanuel College Library.

70 *Ne raorihwadogenhti ne shongwayaner Yesus Keristus, jinihorihoten ne royatado-genhti Matthew.* New York: Young Men's Bible Society of New York, 1831.

This copy of St Matthew's Gospel was translated by Henry Hill (d. 1834) and revised by John A. Wilkes (1807-1836). Hill was an Anglican Mohawk catechist, whose native name was Kenwendeshon. A veteran of the British forces from the War of 1812, he married Christina, the daughter of Joseph Brant, and regularly led Divine Service in the Chapel of the Mohawks, Brantford. Methodist missionaries who lived near the Six Nations encouraged Hill to continue the translation work begun by earlier native leaders like Brant and John Norton. Hill's translation of the Gospel of St Luke appeared in 1828, but because the Methodists were behind the project, Anglican authorities would not promote the use of his books in Canada. After the American Bible Society lost interest in Mohawk translation projects, the cause was taken up by the Young Men's Bible Society of New York, an auxiliary to the Methodist Episcopal Church in the United States. They saw to the translation of the rest of the New Testament (with the exception of II Corinthians) between

1831 and 1836, with the bulk of the work undertaken by Hill. In fact, Hill is generally credited with the majority of Mohawk Scriptural translations, although his name does not always appear on the title pages of the publications themselves. John Wilkes, who came to Canada as a child in 1820, was a school master in Brantford and proficient in the Mohawk tongue. He assisted in the translation and correction of most Mohawk Biblical texts published by the Young Men's Bible Society.

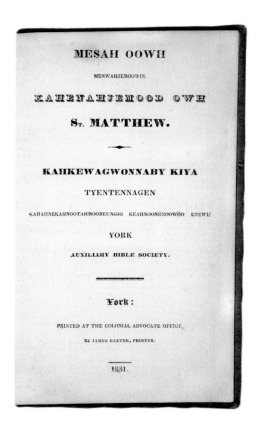

71 *Mesah oowh menwahjemoowin, kahenahjemood owh St. Matthew.* York [Upper Canada]: Printed at the Colonial Advocate Office, 1831.

The King James Version of the Bible served as the immediate source of translation for all projects sponsored by the British and Foreign Bible Society, including this Ojibwa edition published by the York Bible Society in 1831. Owing to royal licensing regulations for the British Empire, the King James text could not be printed alongside the native translation, as had been the case with American imprints. The York Bible Society, which had been founded in November 1818 as 'The Bible Society of Upper Canada', was an interdenominational Protestant association of some of the most powerful men in the young colony. At the time that this book was printed William Baldwin (1775-1844), Robert Baldwin (1804-1858), Jesse Ketchum (1782-1867), Alexander Burnside (1781-1854), and Thomas Morrison (1796-1856) were sitting members, operating under the patronage of the Lieutenant-Governor. The Ojibwa were among the last of the aboriginal peoples in Canada to obtain books written in their own language. Methodist missionaries James Evans (1801-1846) and Peter Jones (1802-1856) competed to supply the need, with Jones providing a partial translation of St Matthew's Gospel in 1829, completing the task in 1831. Jones, whose native name was 'Kahkewaquonaby', was of Welsh and Ojibwa parentage, and a member of the Mississauga tribe. His journals describe his occasionally frustrating interaction with the Bible Society on this particular project. On 4 January 1831, for example, he notes that he 'spent part of the day in trying to get the sub-committee appointed by the York Bible Society for obtaining Indian translations to meet, and to give me some understanding when my translations would be printed'. Jones's missionary work took him to England later in 1831, leaving the correction and revision of *St Matthew* to his brother, the school master John Jones or 'Tyantenagen' (1798-1847). The British and Foreign Bible Society encouraged him to redouble his efforts and complete the New Testament, being 'paid in proportion to what has before been allowed by the Committee for translations of the New Testament'. This volume was printed by James Baxter (1808-1832), the brother-in-law of William Lyon Mackenzie (1795-1861).

72 *The Productions of the Evangelists and Apostles: a Faithful and True Translation of the Scriptures of the New Testament.* Toronto: William Lyon Mackenzie, 1837.

As the centuries passed, and the language and inaccuracies contained within the King James Bible became more troublesome for scholars and readers, an increasing number of new translations began to appear, particularly in the United States. A feeling was growing there that the old version of the Scriptures did not resonate in the New World, and so men like Noah Webster (1758-1843) and Abner Kneeland (1774-1844) tried their hands at providing more exact and accessible translations. In some cases, new translations had become necessary to provide a better dogmatic foundation for growing religious movements like Unitarianism and Mormonism; as a result, language was massaged to allow more favourable interpretations of particular doctrines and practices. In 1826, for example, the Baptist minister Alexander Campbell published a new version of the Scriptures in which the word 'baptize' was consistently replaced with 'immerse', not only better reflecting the original Greek meaning of the word, but also pointing towards accepted Baptist custom. Between 1808 and 1949, some fifty new translations or revisions of the Bible were undertaken in America, and although many were based on the Authorized Version, their relative merits were, in many cases, quite dubious. Among these was this translation by Rodolphus Dickinson (1787-1863), an Episcopal priest from South Carolina. He first published his text at Boston in 1833 and it is remarkable for being among the poorest of the lot. The essential problem is that the translation, while perhaps accurate, is awkward in the extreme. The preface to his New Testament, for example, contains one sentence containing 601 words with eighty-six commas. While the page layout is revolutionary, since it is printed as a narrative with the noticeable absence of chapters and verses, the text itself lacks grace and cadence, and does not flow trippingly off the tongue. The story of the Visitation of Mary to her cousin Elizabeth in the first chapter of Luke, for example, sounds more like a gynecological report. Whereas the King James Version relates that

when Elizabeth heard Mary's greeting 'the babe leapt in her womb', Dickinson says that 'the embryo was joyfully agitated'. William Lyon Mackenzie printed this copy from stereotype plates at Toronto in the same year that he led the Rebellion in Upper Canada. In December of 1836 he had advertised that he was about to publish 'the first Canadian edition' of the Holy Bible. Instead, he printed Dickinson's translation which, since it was not a copy of the Authorized Version, was not bound by any royal copyright laws, and could be printed freely.
On loan from Victoria University - Emmanuel College Library.

73 *The Holy Scriptures, Translated and Corrected by the Spirit of Revelation, by Joseph Smith, Jr., the Seer.* Plano: Church of Jesus Christ of Latter-day Saints, 1867.

In the preface to this book it is explained that Joseph Smith (1805-1844), the founder of the Mormon Church, based his version of the Bible on a 'direct revelation' first received by him in June of 1830. Smith worked on the manuscript until 2 July 1833, and at his death in 1844, the text was entrusted to his wife, Emma Hale (1804-1879). Smith's version purports to include passages that 'had been taken from the Bible, or lost before it was compiled'. Thus, while it uses the King James Bible as its basis, it contains some rather significant revisions, especially in the Book of Genesis, reflecting the theology of the new sect. Emma and her family joined what would become the Reorganized Church of Jesus Christ of Latter Day Saints owing to disagreements with Smith's successor, Brigham Young (1801-1877). In the spring of 1866 a committee of the breakaways proceeded with the publication of Smith's 'translation', while the main Mormon community in Utah continued to use the King James Version. Smith, of course, is better known for *The Book of Mormon* which is described as 'another Testament of Jesus Christ'. First published in 1830 in Palmyra, New York, it was written in a style which clearly imitated the flowing cadences and antique language of the King James Bible. The binding of the first edition was identical to the most common Bibles then supplied by the American Bible Society - brown leather with twin gold bars on the spine, and a black label with gilt lettering.

On loan from the John W. Graham Library, University of Trinity College

74   *The Emphatic Diaglott, containing the Original Greek Text of what is commonly Styled the New Testament.* New York: Fowler and Wells, 1882.

One of the most revolutionary events in modern Biblical studies occurred in 1777 when a professor of New Testament at Jena, Johann Jakob Griesbach (1745-1812), published a new edition of the Greek New Testament. His work was of the utmost significance since it presented the first real challenge to the *Textus Receptus* that had been accepted from the time of Erasmus. Armed with this new critical edition as their source, translators like Benjamin Wilson (as well as Abner Kneeland, Rodolphus Dickinson, and many others) were able to challenge the supremacy of the King James Bible in North America. Described in 1884 as 'notorious', *The Emphatic Diaglott* was first published by Wilson (1817-1900) in 1865 at New York. As the subtitle indicates, the text is printed in Greek with a literal, interlinear English translation of the New Testament, accompanied by a second, narrative form in the margin. This version was closely associated with the early history of the Jehovah's Witnesses who adopted the translation as one of their official texts until the publication of the *New World Translation* in 1950. Among the reasons for this was Wilson's decision to render the Greek word 'Kyrios' or 'Lord' as 'Jehovah' throughout much of the New Testament, as well as his description of the 'coming of Christ' in Matthew as his 'presence', which would help to account for the apparent delay of the Second Coming, which had been predicted for 1874. Using Wilson's translation, the returned Christ could be present, but invisible among believers. After experimenting with several religious traditions, the self-taught Wilson eventually founded the Church of God of the Abrahamic Faith, a sect related to the Christadelphians.

Translations for a Modern World

With so many different English translations of the Bible, beginning with Wycliffe in the fourteenth century, through Tyndale in the sixteenth, right up to recent translations such as the New American Bible, we can genuinely ask ourselves, 'Why are there so many different English versions, and will we still need others in the future?' There are already some four hundred different English renderings of the Bible, in whole or in part. Do we really need more? To answer both questions, we need to appreciate the value and function of translating any text from one language to another.

In the process of translating, we are caught between a rock and a hard place. The Italians have captured the intrinsic problem associated with translation in the phrase '*traduttore traditore*' which simply put means 'a translator is a traitor'; the French similarly observe that '*traduire c'est trahir*' (to translate is to betray). The adages of both cultures highlight the difficult choices translators face when they must choose from among the many nuances offered by the original tongue and the limited alternatives they have in the target language. Translators must choose. And in their choice they interpret the original text for themselves and their audience, for good or for ill.

But, there is another phrase that puts a rather more positive spin on this task, espoused by scholars like Roland Barthes and Umberto Eco: 'Every reading of a text is a new interpretation'. In other words, when we read, we also interpret and 'translate' into our common language. So, even those who read the Bible in the original languages, whether Hebrew, Aramaic, or Greek, are ultimately interpreting the text in the very process of reading. They must constantly choose from among the many nuances offered and opt for the one they wish to emphasize. The original language remains important for maintaining the full range of possible interpretations, but we should not be blind to the fact that a reader is always interpreting, even when a text is studied in the original language. Fundamentally, he or she is translating from one cultural milieu to another.

So why have there been so many English translations? Because there are so many different English language communities which have read the Bible. Will we need new translations in the future? Of course, since each community which values the Bible continues to interpret the Biblical world in its own time. Every reading of the Scriptures, whether in the original language or in translation, is a new interpretation.

The Reverend Michael Kolarcik, s.j.,

Associate Professor of Old Testament, Regis College, University of Toronto

75 *The Holy Bible, Containing the Old and New Testaments, Translated out of the Original Tongues: being the Version Set Forth a.d. 1611, Compared with the most Ancient Authorities and Revised.* Printed for the Universities of Oxford and Cambridge, 1885. (Revised Version.)

With the discovery of previously unknown Greek New Testament manuscripts in the centuries after the Reformation, scholars like Griesbach came to see that the *Textus Receptus* was, in fact, deficient. While this situation may have proved exciting for exegetes, it posed a problem for clergy since this flawed text formed the underlying basis for the King James Bible itself. The origins of the Revised Version can be traced to 1870 when the Convocation of the Province of Canterbury decided that a new edition of the Scriptures was necessary. It was a contentious process from the start, about which little is known since most primary source documents of the period are missing, and the minute books of the meetings yield very little useful information. As with the original project of 1604-1611, the work was to be done by committee, but the result would not be a new translation of the Scriptures so much as a thorough revision. The beloved language would, theoretically, not be altered from the King James Version except when such changes were deemed necessary in the judgment of the most eminent scholars. Furthermore, where such modifications did occur, they were to be executed in the Stuart language of the existing version. The committee's composition was itself subject to controversy since, among other things, non-Anglicans had been invited to participate, including the Roman Catholic convert John Henry Newman (1801-1890), who refused, and the Unitarian scholar G. Vance Smith (1816-1902), whose presence proved to be a source of division. Work progressed nevertheless, and the New Testament appeared in 1881, with the Old Testament following four years later. The excitement at the publication of the New Testament was palpable. One contemporary scholar wrote:

> *The streets around the publishing house in London were blocked from early dawn until late in the afternoon, and there were the same scenes at the great railway termini. A million copies had been called for in England and America. Within a few days nearly four hundred thousand of the Clarendon Press edition had been sold in New York. Two daily papers in Chicago had the work telegraphed to them, and gave it complete in their columns. In less than a year three million copies had been sold.*

In the end, however, the project was not a triumph. While it was extremely popular with academics who praised the greater accuracy of the text and clarity of the prose, for the ordinary Christian, tampering with what had become sacred language was not to be tolerated. To begin with, the text, while versified, was laid out in an unfamiliar paragraph form; more jarring still, however, was the rendering of favourite texts, such as the Lord's Prayer which now read, 'Thy will be done, as in heaven, so on earth'. In the wake of its publication there were threats of law suits, allegations of theft of intellectual property, bidding wars between publishing houses, and charges of heresy. The revision was never truly accepted in the Protestant world. Its reception is best summarized in a 1940 satire in which the following 'vision' is recorded. 'In ye chapel at Ridley Hall', it describes, 'we turned ye lecterne straight. We tooke awaye therefrom .i. superstitiouse booke called ye *Revised Version* & did put ye Bible in place thereof.'

76 *The Bible in Basic English.* Cambridge: University Press in Association with Evans Bros., 1949.

Samuel H. Hooke (1874-1968) was the principal editor of this revolutionary experiment in Biblical translation. Based on the orthological theories of C.K. Ogden (1889-1957) of Cambridge, this Bible renders the sacred text in plain English, stripped of all rhetorical devices. It was welcomed in many quarters throughout the Christian world when the New Testament first appeared in 1941, although concerns were expressed that the process of simplification could lead to misinterpretation. Nevertheless, the intelligibility and compact nature of the text made it popular with ordinary readers. The redactors drew upon only 950 words, with fifty additional 'Biblical' terms not normally found in common usage, to produce a copy of the Scriptures that was especially helpful for those who spoke English as a second language or were intellectually challenged. Hooke, the Anglican priest behind the project, was a professor at the University of London, and has been described as 'a scholar who combined an accurate mastery of Biblical philology and religion with the qualities of spiritual insight not always found in scholars'. During the First World War, he was Flavelle Associate Professor of Oriental Languages and Literature at Victoria College, University of Toronto, where he also taught English and history. As leader of the Student Christian Movement there, his liberal views exerted a powerful, and some claimed inordinate, influence over his students. As a result he was forced to resign from the University in 1925.

77 *New World Translation of the Christian Greek Scriptures.* Brooklyn: Watch-tower Bible and Tract Society, 1950.

This copy of the Scriptures, prepared by and for the use of the Jehovah's Witnesses community, has been controversial from its first appearance in 1950. In keeping with Witness tradition, members of the translation committee remain anonymous. It has been repeatedly charged, however, that their translation methodology did not follow accepted academic standards for such work, but attempted rather to 'foster the distinctive view of a particular sect'. Although it should not be unexpected, one of the most contentious editorial decisions was to employ the word 'Jehovah' for 'Lord' throughout the Bible, including the New Testament, in spite of the fact that the translating committee itself admitted that the use of this title is a mistranslation. Like the Revised Version of 1881, it is printed in paragraphs, and while modern English is used throughout, chosen idioms are often awkward. Reflecting their particular doctrines, 'torture stake' replaces 'cross', and 'impale' is used rather than 'crucify'. In its favour, however, it has been suggested that the translation offers alternative ways of re-imagining a well-known narrative.

78 John Bertram Phillips (1906-1982). *Letters to Young Churches: A Translation of the New Testament Epistles.* London: G. Bles, [1952].

In the preface to this work, C.S. Lewis (1898-1863) explains that by offering another translation of the New Testament Epistles, John Phillips has revealed something of the basic character of the original Greek texts, written as they were, by people for whom Greek was not their mother tongue. The reality of this is often obscured, he claims, by the lofty prose of the Authorized Version and subsequent editions which use it as their common base. 'The same antique glamour which has made it so "beautiful", so "sacred", so "comforting", and so "inspiring" has also made it in many places unintelligible', he complains. Phillips was the Vicar of St

John's, Redhill at the time of this book's first publication in 1947. His intent was not so much to be meticulously accurate, as to convey something of the sense of excitement and urgency that was present in the earliest Greek manuscripts, a feature that can often be overlooked in translation. While generally well-received, Phillips was not without his critics. Arguing for the retention of a certain amount of archaism in Biblical translation, one commentator observed that 'events are not so timeless as ideas, and sometimes a reminder of their background in time and space gives a better understanding of them than if we were encouraged to think of them as if they were contemporary'. For Phillips himself, however, eliciting the immediacy of the Scriptures was a pastoral action that transcended scholarly criticism. His first translations were made to stimulate the enthusiasm of his parish youth group in England, and in the process, he writes, 'I felt like an electrician re-wiring an ancient house, without being able to "turn the mains off."'

79 *The Torah: The Five Books of Moses: A New Translation of the Holy Scriptures according to the Masoretic Text, First Section.* Philadelphia: Jewish Publication Society of America, 1962.

This translation of the Pentateuch by a team of six Hebrew and rabbinical scholars under the direction of Harry M. Orlinsky (1908-1992) was praised upon publication for having captured the shades of meaning in difficult Hebrew words and expressions which had previously been indifferently rendered in English; nevertheless, it was not without its syntactical problems. Reviewers noted that numerous technical and legal terms were clearly mistranslations, while other Hebrew words like 'ephod' (a priestly vestment), for which there is no obvious English equivalent, were unhelpfully left in the original language. It was recognized in the scholarly Jewish community, however, as the best English translation to appear on the market since the beginning of the twentieth century. Orlinsky was a native of Owen Sound, Ontario and a graduate of the University of Toronto who served on the translation team for the *Revised Standard Version of 1952*, the *New Jewish Publication Society of America Version* of 1985, and the *New Revised Standard Version* of 1989.

80 *Good News for Modern Man: The New Testament in Today's English Version.* New York: American Bible Society, 1966.

Until the twentieth century, Biblical translation essentially amounted to a verbatim re-presentation of the sacred text in English. This regard for the literal integrity of the Word, as manifest in the King James or the Douai-Rheims versions of the Bible, occasionally caused the meaning of a passage to become obscure for average readers unfamiliar with the literary conventions of ancient tongues. To redress this situation publications that were essentially paraphrases of the Scriptures such as *The Bible in Basic English and Letters to Young Churches* began to appear. The contribution of translator Robert G. Stratcher of the American Bible Society to this new genre was *Good News for Modern Man*, a copy of the New Testament which stressed the meaning of the text over the form. The result was a version of the Scriptures that avoided the theological language of traditional editions, though often at the expense of accuracy. By unfolding the Biblical narrative in the style of a newspaper report, Stratcher conveyed something of the energy of the moment in language accessible to ordinary readers. Unfortunately, such an approach also communicated some of the stylistic flatness of that medium as well. 'Give us this day our daily bread', for example, becomes 'the food we need', which may actually miss the point of that petition in the Lord's Prayer. Revolutionary in many ways, even the paperback binding featuring headlines from international newspapers was as far removed from a traditional Bible format as could be imagined, and added to the publication's popularity. The initial print-run of 150,000 sold out almost immediately, with some 75 million copies in circulation by 1991.
On loan from the John W. Graham Library, University of Trinity College.

81   *The Holy Bible: New International Version, Containing the Old Testament and the New Testament.* Grand Rapids: Zondervan Bible Publishers, 1978.

Until the recent resurgence in popularity of the King James, the New International Version was the Bible of choice among Evangelical Protestants in the United States. In part, its attractiveness may be attributed to the large translation committee which was composed of Evangelical scholars drawn from all over the English-speaking world. The New Testament appeared in 1973 and was generally well-received, though with some reservations over its more conservative doctrinal approach to the text as well as the translation process itself. With advance sales of 1,200,000, the first printing of the complete Bible in 1978 was the largest ever undertaken for an English copy of the Scriptures. Using the ancient Biblical languages as their translation base, the redactors attempted to produce a Bible that was modern in language while preserving something of the character of the King James tone, so beloved by their Protestant readers. To give some sense of the relative popularity of the respective translations, in 2001 the King James commanded thirty-seven percent of the American market share for Bibles, while the New International Version placed second - with seven percent.

82   *The Holy Bible, containing the Old and New Testaments with the Apocryphal /Deuterocanonical Books.* New York: Oxford University Press, 1989. (New Revised Standard Version.)

Unlike the Good News Bible, the New International Version, and some thirty other English renderings of the Scriptures that have appeared since the middle of the twentieth century, the New Revised Standard Edition traces its pedigree through the Revised Standard Version of 1952 back to the King James Version of 1611. Like these other great monuments of Biblical literature, it is the direct heir of Tyndale. In 1973 the Division of Education and Ministry of the National Council of Churches in the United States initiated a project to produce a Bible that reflected the numerous and significant advances in Biblical scholarship that had been made since the discovery of the Nag Hammadi and Dead Sea Scrolls between 1945 and 1956. It was also recognized that, since the English language is a constantly evolving reality, it was necessary to adapt the classic expressions of the Scriptures in a manner that preserved their poetry and resonance while better expressing modern English idiom. Like its predecessors, the revision was done by a committee of scholars; unlike previous efforts, however, membership included men and women from the Roman Catholic, Protestant, Eastern Orthodox, and Jewish communities making this the most diverse and inclusive body ever to have undertaken a Biblical translation in common. While archaic syntax was elimi-nated, every effort was made to preserve the flavour of expression that originated with Tyndale. More controversial, however, was the effort to eradicate the mas-culine-oriented language from the text wherever possible, while still preserving the patriarchal context of the Scriptures themselves. This proved to be especially vexatious for more conservative religious communities who rejected, for example, the decision to add the word 'sisters' to Paul's salutation to the brethren, since it is not found in the original Greek text. While the NRSV is commonly used during worship in the mainstream Protestant churches throughout the English-speaking world, it has not achieved similar popularity within either the Roman Catholic or Orthodox communities. An adapted form was approved for use by the Canadian Conference of Catholic Bishops in 2007, making Canada the only nation to have a Catholic lectionary based on the NRSV.

On loan from a private collection.

83 *The Saint John's Bible.* Heritage Edition. Collegeville, Minnesota: Saint John's Bible, 2009. (New Revised Standard Version.)

On Ash Wednesday, 8 March 2000, the first sentence of the magnificent Saint

John's manuscript Bible - 'In the beginning was the Word' - was penned by the Queen's calligrapher, Donald Jackson, for St John's Abbey, a Benedictine monastery in central Minnesota. The original manuscript, which has taken almost ten years to write and illuminate, was executed using materials that would have been entirely familiar to the medieval monk. Calf-skin vellum, goose, and swan quills for the lettering, lamp-black ink, natural pigments, gold and silver leaf - these are just some of the components that have gone into the making of this modern masterpiece. By the time the project is concluded, some 250 skins will have been employed for 1,150 pages. A committee of theologians, art historians, Biblical scholars, and artists determined which texts required special artistic attention, with their principal focus on the Benedictine themes of hospitality, conversion of life, and justice. The base text is the New Revised Standard Version, which ironically is not permitted for use in Catholic worship in the United States. In the end, five scribes collaborated with Jackson on the project, and given the sheer magnitude, it is arguably without any rival in scope and extent since the invention of the printing press in the mid-fifteenth century. Copies of the original multi-volume manuscript, which is housed at the Abbey, have been made for the general public. On display is one volume of the 'Heritage Edition', a very limited, extraordinarily high quality reproduction through which, the Abbey hopes 'communities around the world can use this gift of sacred art to ignite their spiritual imaginations for generations to come'.

On loan from Regis College, Toronto.

84 Robert Crumb. *The Book of Genesis Illustrated.* New York: Norton, 2009.

In his introduction to this graphic novel, the artist Robert Crumb informs his readers that he has 'faithfully reproduced every word of the original text, which I derived from several sources, including the King James Version, but mostly from Robert Alter's recent translation, *The Five Books of Moses* (2004)'. Crumb admits that he does not believe the text to be the 'Word of God' in any sense, but rather the creative work of humans which remains 'a powerful text with layers of meaning that reach deep into our collective consciousness.' To say that this project was a departure for Crumb would be an understatement. Better known as a hero of the underground comic book world, responsible for the 'Keep on Truckin' symbol and such characters as the X-rated Fritz the Cat, Crumb predicted that his frank depiction of the Biblical scenes would elicit howls of indignation from the reli-

gious right. Reviewers, however, maintain that his artwork is consistent with the ancient tradition of Biblical illustration and have described it as being 'without a trace of irony, and certainly no mockery . . . a literal - one might even say traditional - rendition of the events in the Judeo-Christian account of Creation and its aftermath'. It is the realism of Crumb's art which has proven to be both effective and affective. As the story of the sacrifice of Isaac unfolds through comic book frames, for example, Crumb captures an old man's growing horror in a way that even the prose of the King James Bible on its own could not fully convey. The translator, Robert Alter, Professor of Hebrew Language and Comparative Literature at the University of California, Berkeley, offered a new translation of the entire Pentateuch because he felt that previous efforts either had a faulty grasp of English or of Hebrew. While admitting his respect for the King James Version with its poetic language and flowing cadences, Alter believed a new attempt was necessary 'to do fuller justice to all these aspects of Biblical style in the hope of making the rich literary experience of the Hebrew more accessible to readers of English'.

On loan from a private collection.

135

Within my Walls
a Memorial

Illuminated Manuscript Leaves

These Scriptural texts are detached from three unidentified later medieval manuscripts. The first leaf contains the concluding verses of Psalm 49 and the beginning of the penitential Psalm 50 (according to the Vulgate numbering), and dates from the late thirteenth century in France. The second leaf comes from a New Testament of British origin, dating from the end of the fourteenth century and includes the end of the fourth chapter of the Gospel of Luke which relates the story of Jesus reading from the Isaiah scroll in the synagogue at Nazareth. The third leaf formed part of a Book of Hours written in France at the beginning of the fifteenth century and includes parts of two of the penitential Psalms, 6 and 31.

Two Leaves from the Bohun Bible

These are but two of the 166 leaves known to have been detached from the magnificent Bohun lectern Bible that was originally made in England - perhaps at Chester - around the middle of the fourteenth century. The artistic style of the manuscript associates its creation with the Bohun family who were the Earls of Hereford and the most important patrons of manuscript illumination at this time. The book itself, however, spent most of its life in Cheshire. Given its size, and the fact that many pages are marked in the margins for liturgical use, the manuscript was probably intended for a church or chapel, and not for private study; further evidence suggests that it was intended for a Carmelite monastery. In its original state the manuscript consisted of 413 leaves, most likely bound in four separate volumes. These were already defective by the end of the seventeenth century, and the books were probably completely dismembered for sale about 1927 by Myers & Co. of

London. On the left is leaf 248 with Jeremiah 50; on the right leaf 324 containing Ezekiel 40.

A Leaf from the Prophet Isaiah – 'Noble Fragments' from the Gutenberg Bible

This page from the 42-line Gutenberg Bible, first printed in Mainz about 1454, comes from a broken copy purchased in 1911 by the New York book dealer Gabriel Wells. In 1911 he began selling individual leaves from the book which are now known as 'Noble Fragments'. Gutenberg's invention of movable type in the middle of the fifteenth century was not simply a technological revolution; it initiated a cultural upheaval that both enhanced the Church's power as well as took direct aim at the institution itself. On the one hand, it meant that the Church was able to disseminate its message much more effectively than it had ever done before. On the other, however, the press posed a threat to the hegemony of the Western Church since, in the words of one scholar, it 'ate inexorably away at that clerical monopoly on sacred knowledge that the Church of Rome was so reluctant to relinquish'. In effect, the Sacred Word became democratized since it no longer belonged only to the very few who had previously made manuscripts or could afford to purchase them. In time it became possible to put copies of the Bible into the hands of the many across Europe whose access to the Scriptures had previously been restricted to what was heard, as read and interpreted by the priest standing in his pulpit. This new technology, therefore, actually jeopardized the communal nature of religion since the Scriptures could now be studied in the privacy of the home. According to the Gutenberg Museum, some forty-eight complete copies of this first printed Bible survive out of the original one hundred and eighty.

On loan from a private collection.

Letter from Colonel John Ready at the Castle of St Lewis to William Lunn, Montreal Concerning the Admission into Canada of Bibles and Testaments Printed Abroad. Quebec: 21 September 1820.

William Lunn (1796-1886) was a businessman, politician, and educator, who was born in Devonport, England and died in Montreal. His most enduring contribution to the life of his adopted city was in the field of education. At a time when instruction for Catholic children was mainly provided by the Church, education for Protestants depended heavily on private schools operated by individual teachers, schools supported by British missionary groups such as the Society for the Propagation of the Gospel, or those promoted by the cooperative efforts of small groups of concerned citizens. One of these cooperative ventures was organized by William Lunn in 1822 when he helped to establish the British and Canadian School Society. Colonel John Ready (d. 1845) was a career officer in the British Army. In 1818 he arrived in Canada as Civil Secretary to the Duke of Richmond, who was Governor-in-Chief of British North America. It was in this capacity that he oversaw the customs bureaucracy for the colony. Since the printing of the King James Bible was restricted within the British Empire to the King's Printer and to the universities of Oxford and Cambridge, all copies of the Scriptures had to be imported into Canada from England. As William Lyon Mackenzie's broadsheet *Beware of Wooden Nutmegs!!* noted, it was still illegal at this time to import copies of the Bible from the United States. This letter informs Lunn of the arrival at the Port of St John's of a shipment of Bibles and Testaments, likely destined for use in his classrooms in Montreal.

S. Thompson's Books! Beware of Wooden Nutmegs!! York, U.C.: William Lyon Mackenzie, 1827.

It is not surprising that Mackenzie would have reacted with such alarm at the efforts of Thompson to introduce into the Canadian market an American sterotype edition of the King James Bible. The production of Bibles had been a lucrative enterprise since the Elizabethan era. Given the royal copyright restrictions associated with its printing, Mackenzie would have been loath to see a competitor gain an advantage in an arena that he could not lawfully participate. Thompson apparently falsely advertised his quarto Bible as the first Canadian copy of the Scriptures to appear in print, which, had it been true would have been illegal since it did not have the necessary royal approbation. Mackenzie accurately identified Thompson's Bibles as American imports, which their Cooperstown, New York imprints eventually bore out. Their importation into Canada was equally unlawful as Mackenzie demonstrates, using chapter and verse from British laws to prove his point. Mackenzie himself would eventually print a copy of the New Testament at Toronto, but it would be Rodophus Dickinson's version (see number 72), not the King James Bible, and therefore not subject to the royal copyright laws. Wenceslaus Hollar (1607-1677)

Seven Days of the Week

These etchings were executed by one of the greatest artists of the seventeenth century, the Bohemian engraver Wenceslaus Hollar (1607-1677). The first set depicts the order of creation as described in the first chapter of the book of Genesis. They first appeared in 1642 in Sir Richard Baker's *Meditations and Motives for Prayer upon the Seaven Dayes of ye Weeke,* printed at London for Richard Royston and Francis Eglesfeild. Similar prints were often inserted into octavo Bibles of the period.

Illustrations to Genesis

This set of etchings narrates the story of the Patriarch Abraham and was originally produced around 1662 from a single copper plate with the etching arranged in four rows of four. Individual illustrations were cut from the sheet and then inserted into octavo Bibles at the time of the Restoration. The plate was apparently preserved and reused in 1753 by John Bowles & Son for an illustrated Genesis.

The Holy Week

These etchings appeared in *The Office of Holy Week according to the Missall and Roman Breviary* printed at Paris in 1670, and reused by Matthew Turner of High Holborn in 1687, a rare example of devotional book expressly intended for the use of English Roman Catholics. The illustrations, faithfully copied from the Dutch engraver Boetius a Bolswert, are often found tipped into Bibles and prayer books of earlier dates. Hollar's original copper plates for this series are preserved in the Bodleian Library.

Bibliography

Allison, Antony Francis & Rogers, D. M. *The Contemporary Printed Literature of the English Counter-Reformation between 1558-1640 : an Annotated Catalogue.* Brookfield, VT : Scolar Press, 1989-1994.

Baker, David W. 'Topical Utopias: Radicalizing Humanism in Sixteenth-Century England", *Studies in English Literature, 1500-1900,* vol. 36, no. 1, The English Renaissance (Winter, 1996), p. 1-30.

Barker, Nicolas. 'The Polyglot Bible', *The Cambridge History of the Book in Britain,* vol. 4. Cambridge : University Press, 1994, p. 648-651.

Bedouelle, Guy. 'The Bible, Printing and the Educational Goals of the Humanists', *The Bible as Book : the First Printed Editions.* London : The British Library & Oak Knoll Press, 1999, p. 95-99.

Bennett, H.S. *English Books & Readers: 1475-1557.* Cambridge: University Press, 1952.

Bennett, H.S. *English Books & Readers: 1558 to 1603.* Cambridge: University Press, 1965.

Bentley, G.E. 'Images of the Word : Separately published English Bible Illustrations, 1539-1830', *Studies in Bibliography,* vol. 47 (1994), p. 103-128.

Betteridge, Maurice S. "The Bitter Notes: The Geneva Bible and its Annotations", *The Sixteenth Century Journal,* vol. 14, no. 1 (1983), p. 41-62.

"Bible Burning" in *The Catholic Layman,* vol. 1, no. 4 (Apr. 1852), p. 41-42.

Bird, T.E. *The Bible in Catholic England.* London: Catholic Truth Society, 1938.

Brake, D.L. *A Visual History of the English Bible.* Grand Rapids: Baker, 2008.

British and Foreign Bible Society. *Historical catalogue of the printed editions of Holy Scripture in the library of the British and Foreign Bible Society.* New York: Kraus Reprint Corp., 1963.

Brown, Michelle P. *The Lindisfarne Gospels: Society, Spirituality and the Scribe.* Toronto: University of Toronto Press, 2003.

Cadwallader, Alan. 'The Politics of Translation of the Revised Version: Evidence from the Newly Discovered Notebooks of Brooke Foss Westcott", *Journal of Theological Studies,* NS, vol. 58, pt. 2 (Oct. 2007), p. 415-439.

Cheek, John L. 'New Testament Translation in America', JBL 72 (1953), p. 103-114.

Craig, Clarence T. "The Revised Standard Version", *Journal of Bible and Religion*, vol. 14, no. 1 (Feb. 1946), p. 33-36.

Crehan, F.J. 'The Bible in the Roman Catholic Church from Trent to the Present Day', *Cambridge History of the Bible.* Cambridge: University Press, 1963, p. 199-237.

Daniell, David. *William Tyndale: A Biography.* New Haven: Yale, 1994.

Daniell, David. *The Bible in English.* New Haven : Yale, 2003.

Dannenfeldt, Karl H. 'The Renaissance Humanists and the Knowledge of Arabic', *Studies in the Renaissance*, vol. 2 (1955), p. 96-117.

Danner, Dan G. "The Contribution of the Geneva Bible of 1560 to the English Protestant Tradition". *Sixteenth Century Journal*, vol. 13, no 3 (1981), p. 5-18.

De Hamel, Christopher. *The Book : a History of the Bible.* London : Phaidon, 2001.

De Hamel, Christopher. 'The Bohun Bible Leaves', *Script & Print*, vol. 32, no. I (2008), p. 49-63.

Duerden, Richard. 'Equivalence or Power? Authority and Reformation Bible Translation', *The Bible as Book : the Reformation.* London : The British Library & Oak Knoll Press, 1999, p. 9-23.

Duffy, Eamon. *The Stripping of the Altars.* New Haven: Yale University Press, 1992.

Edler, Florence. 'Cost Accounting in the Sixteenth Century: The Books of Account of Christopher Plantin, Antwerp, Printer and Publisher', *The Accounting Review*, vol. 12, no. 3 (Sep., 1937), pp. 226-237.

Eisenstein, Elizabeth L. *The Printing Revolution in Early Modern Europe.* Cambridge: University Press, 2005.

Fogarty, Gerald P. *American Catholic Biblical Scholarship: A History from the Early Republic to Vatican II.* New York: Harper & Row, 1989.

Fowler, David C. 'John Trevisa and the English Bible'. *Modern Philology* (1960), p. 81-98.

Fox, Harold G. 'Copyright in Relation to the Crown and Universities with Special Reference to Canada', *The University of Toronto Law Journal*, vol. 7, no. 1 (1947) p. 98-136.

Fuller, Thomas. *The Church-history of Britain, from the Birth of Jesus Christ untill the Year* M.DC.XLVIII. London: John Williams, 1655.

Gilmont, J.-F. English ed. & trans. by Karin Maag. *The Reformation and the Book.* Aldershot : Ashgate, 1998.

Glowacki, David R. 'To the Reader: the Structure of Power in Biblical Translation, from Tyndale to the NRSV', *Literature & Theology* 22, no. 2 (June 2008), p. 195-209.

Goodspeed, E.J. 'The Toronto Gospels', *American Journal of Theology* 15 (1911), p. 268-271, 445-459.

Hall, Basil. 'Biblical Scholarship: Editions and Commentaries,' *Cambridge History of the Bible.* Cambridge: University Press, 1963, p. 38-93.

Hammond, Gerald. 'What was the influence of the Medieval English Bible upon the Renaissance Bible?' *Bulletin of the John Rylands University Library of Manchester* 77, no. 3 (Autumn 1995), p. 87-97.

Hargreaves, Henry. 'The Wycliffite Versions', *Cambridge History of the Bible,* vol. 2. Cambridge: University Press, 1969, p. 387-415.

Hayden, Roger. 'Canne, John (d. 1667?)', *Oxford Dictionary of National Biography,* Oxford : University Press, 2004.

Hayes, T. Wilson. 'The Peaceful Apocalypse: Familism and Literacy in Sixteenth-Century England', *The Sixteenth Century Journal,* vol. 17, no. 2 (Summer, 1986), p. 131-143.

Herbert, A.S. *Historical Catalogue of Printed Editions of the English Bible 1525-1961 : Revised and Expanded from the Edition of T.H. Darlow and H.F. Moule, 1903 . . .* London : British and Foreign Bible Society, 1968.

Holmes, Peter. *Resistance and Compromise : the Political Thought of the Elizabethan Catholics.* Cambridge : University Press, 1982.

Howlett, David R. 'Biblical Style in Early Insular Latin', in *Sources of Anglo-Saxon Literary Culture.* Kalamazoo: University of Michigan Press, 1986.

Hudson, Anne. *Lollards and their Books.* London : The Hambledon Press, 1985.

Hudson, Anne. *The Premature Reformation.* Oxford : Clarendon Press, 1988.

Ing, J. *Johann Gutenberg and his Bible: A Historical Study.* New York: The Typophiles, 1988.

Hughes, Celia. 'Coverdale's Alter Ego', *Bulletin of the John Rylands University Library of Manchester* 65 (Autumn 1982), p. 100-124.

Jenkins, A.K. & Preston, P. *Biblical Scholarship and the Church: A Sixteenth-Century Crisis of*

Authority. Aldershot: Ashgate, 2007.

Jones, G. Lloyd. *The Discovery of Hebrew in Tudor England: a Third Language.* Manchester: University Press, 1983.

Kathman, David. 'Barker, Christopher (1528/9-1599)', *Oxford Dictionary of National Biography,* Oxford University Press, 2004.

Kelly, J. N. D. *Jerome: His Life, Writings, and Controversies.* London: Duckworth, 1975.

King, John N. 'Becke, Edmund (fl. 1549-1551)'. *Oxford Dictionary of National Biography.* Oxford : University Press, 2004.

Krey, Philip D. W. & Smith, Lesley. *Nicholas of Lyra: The Senses of Scripture.* Leiden: Brill, 2000.

Latré, Guido. 'The 1535 Coverdale Bible and its Antwerp origins', *The Bible as Book: the Reformation.* London : The British Library & Oak Knoll Press, 2000, p. 89-102.

Lewis, Jack P. *The English Bible from KJV to NIV: A History and Evaluation.* Grand Rapids: Baker, 1991.

Loewe, Raphael. 'The Medieval History of the Latin Vulgate,' *Cambridge History of the Bible,* vol. 2. Cambridge: University Press, 1969, p. 102-54.

MacMahon, Luke. 'Tomson, Laurence (1539-1608)', *Oxford Dictionary of National Biography.* Oxford : University Press, 2004.

MacSkimming, R. *The Perilous Trade: Publishing Canada's Writers.* Toronto : M&S, 2003.

McGrath, Alister. *In the Beginning: The Story of the King James Bible and how it changed a Nation, a Language, and a Culture.* New York: Anchor Books, 2001.

McMullin, B.J. 'The Bible Trade', *The Cambridge History of the Book in Britain,* vol. 4. Cambridge: University Press, 1994, p. 455-473.

McNally, R.E. "The Council of Trent and Vernacular Bibles", *Theological Studies,* vol. 27 (1966), p. 204-227.

Mihelic, Joseph L. "The Study of Hebrew in England", *Journal of Bible and Religion,* vol. 14, no. 2 (May, 1946), p. 94-100.

Mozley, J.F. *Coverdale and his Bibles.* London : Lutterworth, 1953.

Nees, Lawrence. 'Reading Aldred's Colophon for the Lindisfarne Gospels', *Speculum,* Vol. 78, No. 2 (Apr., 2003), p. 333-377.

Ng, Su Fang. 'Translation, Interpretation, and Heresy: The Wycliffite Bible, Tyndale's Bible, and the Contested Origin'. *Studies in Philology*, vol. 98, no. 3, pp. 315-38, Summer 2001

Nicolson, Adam. *God's Secretaries : the Making of the King James Bible.* New York : Harper Collins, 2003.

Norton, David. 'Imagining translation Committees at Work : the King James and the Revised Versions', *The Bible as Book : the Reformation.* London : The British Library & Oak Knoll Press, 2000, p. 157-168.

Pearson, David. *Books as History. The Importance of Books beyond their Texts.* London: The British Library, 2008.

Pettegree, Andrew. 'Day, John (1521/2-1584)', *Oxford Dictionary of National Biography.* Oxford: University Press, 2004.

Plant, Marjorie. *The English Book Trade. An Economic History of the Making and Sale of Books.* London : Allen & Unwin, 1974.

Pollard, A. W., ed., *Records of the English Bible: the Documents Relating to the Translation and Publication of the Bible in English, 1525-1611* (1911)

Ramsey, Michael. *Canterbury Pilgrim.* London : SPCK, 1974.

Rashkow, Ilona. "Hebrew Translation and the Fear of Judaization", *The Sixteenth Century Journal,* vol. 21, no. 2 (Summer 1990), p. 217-233.

Rekers, B. *Benito Arias Montano (1527-1598).* London: Warburg Institute, 1972.

Richardson, William. 'Boys, John', *Oxford Dictionary of National Biography.* Oxford : University Press, 2004.

Rivers, Isabel. 'Doddridge, Philip', *Oxford Dictionary of National Biography.* Oxford : University Press, 2004.

Royal Ontario Museum. *The Art of Fine Printing and its Influence upon the Bible in Print.* [Toronto : Royal Ontario Museum, 1956].

Saenger, P. 'The Impact of the Early Printed Page on the Reading of the Bible', *The Bible as Book : the First Printed Editions.* London : The British Library & Oak Knoll Press, 1999, p. 31-51.

Sherman, William H. ' "The Book thus Put in Every Vulgar Hand" : Impressions of Readers in Early English Printed Bibles', *The Bible as Book: the First Printed Editions.* London: The British Library & Oak Knoll Press, 1999, p. 125-131.

Shields, R.A. & Forse, J.H. 'Creating the Image of a Martyr: John Porter, Bible Reader", *The Sicteenth Century Journal*, vol. 33, no. 3 (Autumn, 2002), p. 725-734.

Slights, William W.E. '"Marginall notes that spoile the text": Scriptural Annotation in the English Renaissance', *The Huntington Library Quarterly*, vol. 55, number 2 (Spring 1992), p. 255-278.

Southern, A.C. *Elizabethan Recusant Prose 1559-1582.* London : Sands, & Co., 1950.

Stapleton, Matthew P. 'Catholic Bible Translations', *Journal of Bible and Religion*, vol. 14, no. 4 (Nov. 1946), p. 198-202.

String, Tatiana. 'Politics and Polemics in English and German Bible Illustrations', *The Bible as Book : the Reformation.* London : The British Library & Oak Knoll Press, 2000, p. 137-143.

Tedder, H.R. 'Bagster, Samuel, the Elder (1772-1851)', rev. J.M. Alter, *Oxford Dictionary of National Biography.* Oxford : University Press, 2004

Tedder, H. R. 'Jugge, Richard (c.1514-1577)', rev. *Oxford Dictionary of National Biography.* Oxford : University Press, 2004.

Thomas M. McCoog, 'Martin, Gregory (1542?-1582)', *Oxford Dictionary of National Biography,* Oxford University Press, 2004.

Tkacz, Catherine Brown. "Labor Tam Utilis': The Creation of the Vulgate' in *Vigiliae Christianae* 50, no. 1 (1996), p. 42-72.

Tribble, Evelyn B. *Margins and Marginality.* Charlottesville : University Press of Virginia, 1993.

Vikan, Gary ed. *Illuminated Greek Manuscripts from American Collections: An Exhibition in Honor of Kurt Weitzmann.* Princeton: University Press, 1973.

Walsham, Alexandra. 'Unclasping the Book? Post-Reformation English Catholicism and the Vernacular Bible', *Journal of British Studies* 42 (April 2003), p. 141-166.

Welte, M. 'The Problem of the Manuscript Basis for the Earliest Printed Editions of the Greek New Testament', *The Bible as Book : the First Printed Editions.* London : The British Library & Oak Knoll Press, 1999, p. 117-123.

Williams, D.H. 'Scripture, Tradition, and the Church: Reformation and Post-Reformation' in Williams, D.H. *The Free Church and the Early Church.* Grand Rapids : Eerdmans, 2002.